Praise for *uncovered editions*

"The repackaging of classics is a tried and trusted winner, but Tim Coates has come up with something entirely original: the repackaging of history. His **uncovered editions** *collect papers from the archive of The Stationery Office into verbatim narratives, so, for instance, in* UFOs *in the House of Lords we get a hilarious recreation, directly from Hansard, of a nutty debate that took place in 1979 . . . This is inspired publishing, not only archivally valuable but capable of bringing the past back to life without the usual filter of academic or biographer."* **Guardian**

"The Irish Uprising *is a little treasure of a book and anyone with an interest in Irish history will really enjoy it. Its structure is extremely unusual as it is compiled from historic official reports published by the British government from 1914 to 1920 . . . For anyone studying this period of history* The Irish Uprising *is a must as the correspondence and accounts within it are extremely illuminating and the subtle nuances of meaning can be teased out of the terms and phrasing to be more revelatory than the actual words themselves."* **Irish Press, Belfast**

"Voyeurs of all ages will enjoy the original text of the Denning report on Profumo. It is infinitely superior to the film version of the scandal, containing such gems as: 'One night I was invited to a dinner party at the home of a very, very rich man. After I arrived, I discovered it was rather an unusual dinner party. All the guests had taken off their clothes . . . The most intriguing person was a man with a black mask over his face. At first I thought this was a party gimmick. But the truth was that this man is so well known and holds such a responsible position that he did not want to be associated with anything improper.'" **Times Higher Education Supplement**

"Very good to read . . . insight into important things . . . inexorably moving . . . If you want to read about the Titanic, *you won't read a better thing . . . a revelation."* **Open Book, BBC Radio 4**

"Congratulations to The Stationery Office for unearthing and reissuing such an enjoyable vignette" [on Wilfrid Blunt's Egyptian Garden] **The Spectator**

uncovered editions
www.uncovered-editions.co.uk

Series editor: Tim Coates
Managing editor: Michele Staple

New titles in the series
The Assassination of John F. Kennedy, 1963
Attack on Pearl Harbor, 1941
The Cuban Missile Crisis, 1962
Letters of Henry VIII, 1526–29
Mr Hosie's Journey to Tibet, 1904
The St Valentine's Day Massacre, 1929
The Trials of Oscar Wilde, 1895
UFOs in America, 1947

Already published
The Amritsar Massacre: General Dyer in the Punjab, 1919
Bloody Sunday, 1972: Lord Widgery's Report
The Boer War: Ladysmith and Mafeking, 1900
British Battles of World War I, 1914–15
The British Invasion of Tibet: Colonel Younghusband, 1904
Defeat at Gallipoli: the Dardanelles Commission Part II, 1915–16
D Day to VE Day: General Eisenhower's Report, 1944–45
Escape from Germany, 1939–45
Florence Nightingale and the Crimea, 1854–55
The Irish Uprising, 1914–21
John Profumo and Christine Keeler, 1963
The Judgment of Nuremberg, 1946
King Guezo of Dahomey, 1850–52
Lord Kitchener and Winston Churchill: The Dardanelles Commission
    Part I, 1914–15
The Loss of the Titanic, 1912
R.101: the Airship Disaster, 1930
Rillington Place, 1949
The Russian Revolution, 1917
The Siege of Kars, 1855
The Siege of the Peking Embassy, 1900
The Strange Story of Adolf Beck
Tragedy at Bethnal Green
Travels in Mongolia, 1902
UFOs in the House of Lords, 1979
War in the Falklands, 1982
War 1914: Punishing the Serbs
War 1939: Dealing with Adolf Hitler
Wilfrid Blunt's Egyptian Garden: Fox-hunting in Cairo

uncovered editions

THE WATERGATE AFFAIR, 1972

THE RESIGNATION OF PRESIDENT RICHARD M. NIXON

∞◦◦⬦◦◦∞

London: The Stationery Office

© The Stationery Office 2001

Applications for reproduction should be made in writing
to The Stationery Office Limited, St Crispins, Duke
Street, Norwich NR3 1PD.

ISBN 0 11 702747 2
Extracted from the *Watergate Special Prosecution Force
Report, October 1975*, available under the terms of the
Freedom of Information Act.

A CIP catalogue record for this book is available from the
British Library.

Cover photograph shows Richard Nixon in 1974.
© Hulton Archive.

Typeset by J&L Composition Ltd, Filey, North Yorkshire.
Printed in the United Kingdom by The Stationery Office,
London.
TJ5494 C30 10/01

CONTENTS

About the series

Uncovered editions are historic official papers which have not previously been available in a popular form, and have been chosen for the quality of their story-telling. Some subjects are familiar, but others are less well known. Each is a moment in history.

About the series editor, Tim Coates

Tim Coates studied at University College, Oxford and at the University of Stirling. After working in the theatre for a number of years, he took up bookselling and became managing director, firstly of Sherratt and Hughes bookshops, and then of Waterstone's. He is known for his support for foreign literature, particularly from the Czech Republic. The idea for *uncovered editions* came while searching through the bookshelves of his late father-in-law, Air Commodore Patrick Cave, OBE. He is married to Bridget Cave, has two sons, and lives in London.

Tim Coates welcomes views and ideas on the *uncovered editions* series. He can be e-mailed at timcoates@theso.co.uk

LIST OF PERSONS

ANDREAS, DWAYNE, Chairman, First Oceanic Corporation

BABCOCK, TIM, executive of Occidental Petroleum Corporation

BARKER, BERNARD, real estate agent; Watergate burglar

BORK, ROBERT, former Solicitor General; Acting Attorney General

BUZHARDT, FRED, White House counsel

CHAPIN, DWIGHT, Presidential aide

COLSON, CHARLES, special counsel to the President

CONNALLY, JOHN, former Secretary of the Treasury

COX, ARCHIBALD, Special Prosecutor, May 25–October 29, 1973

DEAN, JOHN, former White House counsel

DEDIEGO, FELIPE, real estate agent; Watergate burglar

EHRLICHMAN, JOHN, assistant for domestic affairs; directed "Plumbers" unit

ELLSBERG, DANIEL, defense analyst; leaked the Pentagon Papers

ERVIN, SENATOR SAM J. JR, chairman of Select Committee on Presidential Campaign Activities

FIELDING, DR, Los Angeles psychiatrist

FORD, GERALD, President of the United States of America, 1974–1977

GESSEL, GERHARD, District Judge

GONZALEZ, VIRGILIO, locksmith; Watergate burglar

HAIG, GENERAL ALEXANDER, President's chief of staff

HALDEMAN, H. R., former White House chief of staff

HUNT, E. HOWARD, consultant to White House; involved with "Plumbers" unit; Watergate burglar

JACOBSEN, JAKE, Texas attorney, retained by AMPI

JAWORSKI, LEON, Special Prosecutor, November 1, 1973–October 26, 1974

KALMBACH, HERBERT, former personal lawyer to President Nixon

KLEINDIENST, RICHARD, former Attorney General

KROGH, EGIL, JR, White House aide involved with the "Plumbers" unit

LARUE, FRED, former campaign official

LIDDY, GORDON, former FBI agent, involved with the "Plumbers" unit; Watergate burglar

MAGRUDER, JEB, President Nixon's campaign director

MARTINEZ, EUGENIO, real estate agent; Watergate burglar

McCORD, JAMES W., security coordinator for President Nixon's re-election committee; Watergate burglar

MITCHELL, JOHN, former member of President Nixon's cabinet

NADER, RALPH, US lawyer; campaigner for consumer rights

NIXON, RICHARD, President of the United States of America, January 20, 1969–August 9, 1974

PETERSEN, HENRY, Assistant Attorney General

RICHARDSON, ELLIOT, Attorney General; resigned October 20, 1973

RUCKELSHAUS, WILLIAM, Deputy Attorney General; resigned October 20, 1973

RUTH, HENRY, Deputy Special Prosecutor

SAXBE, WILLIAM, Attorney General

SEGRETTI, DONALD, California lawyer, director of "dirty tricks" operation

SIRICA, JOHN J., Chief Judge of the US District Court for the District of Columbia

ST CLAIR, JAMES, chief counsel to President Nixon for Watergate-related matters

STANS, MAURICE, former Secretary of Commerce; former chairman of FCRP

STEINBRENNER, GEORGE, Chairman, American Ship Building Company

STRACHAN, GORDON, former White House aide

STURGIS, FRANK, ex-Marine; Watergate burglar

VESCO, ROBERT, financier

WOODS, ROSE MARY, secretary to President Nixon

WRIGHT, CHARLES ALAN, consultant to the White House counsel's office

GLOSSARY

AMPI	Associated Milk Producers, Inc.
antitrust	Regulating or preventing trusts or other monopolies, to promote fair competition in business
CIA	Central Intelligence Agency
CRP	Committee to Re-Elect the President
FBI	Federal Bureau of Investigation
FCRP	Finance Committee to Re-Elect the President
FEA	Federation of Experienced Americans
GAO	General Accounting Office
grand jury	A jury of between 12 and 23 persons selected to inquire into accusations of crime, to ascertain whether the evidence is adequate to found an indictment
impeachment	To charge the holder of a public office with high crime
indictment	A formal written charge or accusation of a serious crime
IRS	Internal Revenue Service
ITT	International Telephone and Telegraph Corporation
Pentagon Papers	Documentary history tracing involvement of US in war in Southeast Asia
"Plumbers" unit	Informal name for the Special Investigations

	Unit at the White House, created by President Nixon in 1971 to plug news leaks
Saturday Night Massacre	Resignations of Attorney General Richardson and Deputy Attorney General Ruckelhaus for refusing to fire Special Prosecutor Cox, leading to President Nixon's naming of Robert Bork as new Attorney General, who carried out Nixon's order to fire Cox
SBA	Small Business Administration
SEC	Securities and Exchange Commission
subpoena	A writ requiring appearance in court to give testimony; to serve or summon with such a writ
subpoena duces tecum	A writ requiring a witness to attend court and bring certain documents
Townhouse	Informal name for secret program, sponsored by the White House, for raising and disbursing funds for congressional candidates
writ of mandamus	Judicial writ or order issued in the name of the Government directing an inferior court, corporation, officer etc. to perform a statutory or public duty
WSPF	Watergate Special Prosecution Force

Richard M. Nixon resigned the office of the President of the United States of America on August 9, 1974, during his second term of office. This book quotes selected extracts from the judicial inquiry which led directly to his resignation—a resignation that was necessary as a consequence of illegal acts and attempts to hide those acts from the public and from prosecution.

On May 28, 1972, the Democratic National Committee headquarters in the Watergate complex were broken into and electronic surveillance equipment installed. On June 17, 1972, a team of men were arrested at the headquarters while attempting to repair electronic equipment. On March 19, 1973, one of the convicted men claimed, via letter, in open court that Government witnesses had committed perjury during his trial.

The Watergate Special Prosecution Force, under the leadership of a Special Prosecutor, was set up in May 1973 to investigate the Watergate break-in and cover-up, and other allegations including perjury; activities of the White House "Plumbers" group; "dirty tricks" campaigns; and illegal financing of various Presidential re-election campaigns in 1972.

The Watergate Special Prosecution Report, of October 1975, revealed an extent of abuse of power which astonished the world as it emerged, firstly, in the newspapers of the United States of America, and then in the worldwide press. The report also showed the extent of power which was brought to bear to pursue the aims of those involved, and consequently the enormous courage of those, some of whom feature in this book, who pledged to apply the justice that is assumed in a democracy.

The following extracts from the Watergate Special Prosecution Report relate, from contemporary documents, what happened, and the tortuous investigations that led to these findings. The full reports of the Special Prosecutor's office are lengthy and complete, in that they explain the legal process and reasoning, in a more exact manner than remains in this selection. They also make technical legal recommendations, and fully describe individual cases, neither of which have been included here.

The editor's intention is merely to offer an account, from the official record, of one of the most amazing collections of public crime in the history of democratic government.

INTRODUCTION

The Watergate Special Prosecution Force (WSPF) had, at the time that this report was written, worked for 28 months as an independent investigatory and prosecutive agency within the Department of Justice of the United States of America. As a result of its work, judges and juries had applied the criminal sanction to an unprecedented number of high Government officials and to important business leaders. The Special Prosecutor's mandate included the requirement that he should report to the public and to Congress about his activities.

Some of the task still lay ahead. Appeals would proceed for probably two years or more. A few cases had to be completed. But most of the work of the office was done and most of the staff had finished their tasks. It now seemed appropriate to summarize the completed work in a comprehensive report.

No group of prosecutors and supporting personnel ever have labored under greater public scrutiny. Every decision seemed to be a delicate one and previously uncharted courses frequently had to be faced. Each action occurred in the midst of a national turmoil and, in retrospect, some may be judged in the future as just plain wrong. This report seeks not to justify, but to explain. The Congress, the American people and other law enforcement agencies gave continued support to the efforts of this office. A full accounting, within the confines and strictures that the law properly places upon prosecutors, is required.

*   *   *   *   *

The following report attempts to describe accurately and completely the policies and operations of the Watergate Special Prosecution Force from May 29, 1973 to the middle of September 1975. The chapters of the main report contain a narrative of operations, summaries of major investigations, a narrative of relations with the White House during the Nixon and Ford Administrations, and observations.

BRIEF HISTORY OF THE
WATERGATE SPECIAL
PROSECUTION FORCE

BACKGROUND AND ESTABLISHMENT OF OFFICE

Agents of the Committee to Re-Elect the President (CRP) broke into the Democratic National Committee headquarters in the Watergate office complex on June 17, 1972. The resulting conspiracy, burglary, and wiretapping charges produced convictions of seven men the following January in a trial before Chief Judge John J. Sirica of the US District Court for the District of Columbia. By that time various public allegations had created suspicions that high-level officials of CRP and the Nixon Administration had engaged in a variety of illegal activities connected with the 1972 campaign, of which the Watergate break-in was only one. As a result, the Senate established its Select Committee on Presidential Campaign Activities, chaired by Senator Sam J. Ervin, Jr.

On March 19, 1973, before the Select Committee hearings started, James W. McCord, one of the convicted Watergate burglars, wrote an explosive letter to Judge Sirica who was to sentence him four days later. McCord's letter, revealed in open court, claimed that Government witnesses had committed perjury during his trial and that the trial had failed to identify others involved in the Watergate operation. Throughout April, news accounts based on the reopening of the criminal investigation, the initial Select Committee inquiries and press investigations— as well as public statements by the Administration— increased public doubt about the conduct of high White House and campaign officials. These doubts heightened at the end of April with the dismissal of the counsel to the President, and the resignation of the Attorney General, the acting director of the Federal Bureau of Investigation (FBI), and two of the President's closest aides. Further public concern arose about the desirability of the US Attorney's office continuing its investigation, especially in light of publicly assumed interference from Justice Department and White House officials. During his confirmation hearings before the Senate Judiciary Committee, the newly designated Attorney General, Elliot Richardson, pledged to appoint an independent special prosecutor to take over the inquiry.

With the approval of the Judiciary Committee, Richardson and Archibald Cox, his ultimate choice for the post of Special Prosecutor, agreed upon the terms of Cox's charter. The resulting statement, entitled "Duties and Responsibilities of the Special Prosecutor," became part of

Department of Justice regulations and defined the Special Prosecutor's jurisdiction in these terms:

> The Special Prosecutor shall have full authority for investigating and prosecuting offenses arising out of the unauthorized entry into Democratic National Committee headquarters at the Watergate, all offenses arising out of the 1972 presidential election for which the Special Prosecutor deems it necessary and appropriate to assume responsibility, allegations involving the President, members of the White House staff, or presidential appointees, and any other matters which he consents to have assigned to him by the Attorney General.

Richardson also pledged to Cox adequate funding, complete independence in hiring and supervising his staff, and sole responsibility for contesting any "executive privilege" or "national security" claims which might be raised to prevent the acquisition of evidence. Cox should decide whether to seek grants of immunity (subject to the Attorney General's approval as required by statute), and whether and to what extent he would inform or consult with the Attorney General about his work. Richardson further agreed that he would not "countermand or interfere with the Special Prosecutor's decisions or actions," and that he could remove Cox from office only for "extraordinary improprieties." On May 25, 1973, Cox was sworn in as Special Prosecutor and the Watergate Special Prosecution Force (WSPF) was officially established within the Department of Justice.

MAY 25–OCTOBER 20, 1973

Richardson had told the Senate Judiciary Committee that Cox's jurisdiction would include the Watergate case, the activities of alleged political saboteur Donald Segretti, the office burglary of Dr Lewis Fielding, Daniel Ellsberg's psychiatrist, and illegal activity involving 1972 campaign contributions that Cox chose to investigate. Richardson later referred to Cox certain allegations, including possible perjury in Senate hearings relating to Administration handling of an antitrust suit against the International Telephone and Telegraph Corporation (ITT). When the Justice Department's Criminal and Tax Divisions were conducting any investigations regarding matters related to his jurisdiction, they would inform the Special Prosecutor and ascertain if he wanted to take responsibility. In addition, after initial discussions and inquiries, the Special Prosecutor arranged to see the FBI for investigative work and to send investigative requests directly to the Bureau without transmittal through the Attorney General.[1]

One of Cox's first problems was the possible impact on his work of the Senate Select Committee's televised hearings, which had begun about a week before he took office. Although the Committee and the Special Prosecutor's office were investigating many of the same allegations about Watergate and other Nixon Administration activities, each meant to use the information it would gather for a different purpose, in accord with its particular responsibilities. The Committee sought to bring facts before the public in order to propose legislative remedies for any abuses it might uncover; the Special Prosecutor had the responsibility

---

1. Richardson and Cox also made an agreement as to the prosecution of former Administration officials and others on charges relating to favorable treatment of financier Robert Vesco in return for a campaign contribution. While the matter was within the Special Prosecutor's jurisdiction, Cox agreed that it should continue to be handled by the US Attorney's office for the Southern District of New York, which had conducted the investigation and obtained the indictment in the case. Thereafter, WSPF exercised very little supervisory authority over the case.

of investigating and prosecuting specific criminal charges. The danger existed that legislative hearings might frustrate the criminal proceedings. For example, in order to obtain the testimony of several important witnesses, the Committee planned to immunize them, thus barring any prosecution that could be shown to be based on any direct or indirect use of their Senate testimony. In addition, the televised hearings might create adverse publicity about potential defendants in criminal trials, especially a Watergate trial that then seemed likely to begin in a few months. For these reasons, Cox requested that the Committee postpone its hearings; the Committee quickly rejected this request.

Before two Committee witnesses were immunized, Cox acted to reduce the chance that a future criminal case against either of them would be "tainted" by evidence obtained as a result of their testimony. He arranged to have the evidence already gathered against each of them deposited under seal with the District Court before they testified at the Committee hearings. And, to minimize possible pretrial publicity and ensure maximum fairness to potential defendants, he sought a court order that the Committee's grants of immunity be conditioned on its holding hearings in executive session, or at least without radio and television coverage. However, Judge Sirica concluded that he had no power to issue such an order to a Congressional committee, and Cox decided not to appeal the decision, since a prolonged conflict with the Committee would have kept both groups from their investigative work and the likelihood of a successful appeal was doubtful. In the end, the continuation of public hearings through the summer of 1973, among other benefits, brought to public attention testimony relating to alleged White House involvement in the Watergate cover-up and other crimes and thereby helped create for the Special

Prosecutor's investigation a base of public and Congressional support that did much to force the re-establishment of WSPF after the President's attempt to abolish it later that year.

This early conflict over the possible harm that the Committee's televised hearings would inflict on the cover-up investigation soon subsided. In other WSPF matters, the Committee's staff had commenced its investigation some months before the prosecutors were appointed and had gathered much information of value to WSPF. Most of this information was placed on computer tapes, which the Committee agreed to provide to the prosecutors.[2] WSPF decided to undertake a similar computer operation, and arranged to use the same Library of Congress computer system so that information gathered from other sources could be cross-referenced with that obtained by the Committee.

Meanwhile, Cox was selecting a staff that eventually numbered, in permanent positions, 37 attorneys, 16 other professionals, and 32 supporting personnel by August 1974.[3] The bulk of the investigative work was divided among five task forces, each responsible for a broad area of investigation—the Watergate break-in and cover-up; the allegations about ITT and possible perjury during 1972 Senate hearings; the activities of the White House "Plumbers" group, including the break-in at Ellsberg's psychiatrist's office;[4] Segretti's activities and other alleged

---

2. While the initial agreement between the Committee and the Special Prosecutor had covered only information made public at the Committee's hearings, the Committee agreed in March 1974 to provide WSPF with computer access to other information its staff had gathered which had not been disclosed in hearings.

3. In addition, there were 10 temporary employees at that time.

4. This task force also looked into various alleged abuses related to Federal agencies and later into possible illegal activity in connection with President Nixon's tax returns.

campaign "dirty tricks"; and illegal conduct in the financing of the various Presidential campaigns of 1972.

Assisting and providing support for the task forces were several other groups. A counsel's office was established to provide legal advice to the Special Prosecutor and the task forces. An information section went to work summarizing and cross-indexing the masses of Congressional and grand jury testimony that had already been gathered, and creating a filing and reference system that would give any WSPF investigator access to whatever information was already available in the area of his inquiry. An office of public affairs handled relations with the press—an especially sensitive task in view of the dual demands of the First Amendment's free-press guarantees and the right of a potential defendant to a trial unprejudiced by publicity about his conduct. An administrative office dealt with the many problems of space allocation, payroll, supplies, equipment, clerical help, and messenger service. The FBI and IRS supplied personnel who worked closely with WSPF in some of its investigations, while the Federal Protective Service provided security services for WSPF's offices in a private building in downtown Washington.

The Assistant US Attorneys who had handled the initial Watergate investigation—Earl Silbert, Seymour Glanzer, and Donald Campbell—worked with WSPF until the end of June, when they returned to the US Attorney's office for the District of Columbia. The grand jury that had brought the original Watergate indictment in the fall of 1972, and had received new evidence in the spring of 1973, continued to hear evidence gathered by WSPF in the Watergate cover-up case. In August a second grand jury was empaneled to hear evidence in other cases, and a third grand jury was added in January 1974. Because the original grand jury was so familiar with the Watergate case, special legislation in December 1973 extended its term beyond the normal 18 months.

As the various task forces were absorbing information already gathered by other investigators and beginning to interview witnesses and bring them before the grand jury, the Senate Select Committee continued its hearings. In June, former White House counsel John Dean gave testimony implicating President Nixon and his closest advisers in the Watergate cover-up. On July 16, a former White House official told the Committee that President Nixon in 1971 had installed in the White House a taping system designed to record his meetings and telephone conversations. This revelation opened up the possibility of obtaining evidence that could resolve the conflicting testimony about alleged involvement of Administration officials in various crimes.

On July 23, the Special Prosecutor, after unsuccessful attempts to obtain such material from the President on a voluntary basis, issued a subpoena on behalf of the grand jury for the tapes, notes, and memoranda of nine conversations which the available evidence indicated were relevant and necessary to the investigation. The President opposed the subpoena, and appealed Judge Sirica's order enforcing it to the US Court of Appeals for the District of Columbia Circuit. After first suggesting that Cox and the White House seek a compromise—which they were unable to do—the appellate court on October 12 affirmed Judge Sirica's order with modifications sought by the Special Prosecutor. The Court directed Judge Sirica to listen to the tapes to determine whether they contained discussions subject to a valid claim of executive privilege, and then turn over any unprivileged sections of the tapes to the grand jury.

While the litigation over the subpoenaed tapes had delayed the Watergate and other WSPF investigations, the prosecutors had made considerable progress in the first six months of their work. The Watergate investigation had produced guilty pleas from Fred LaRue, Jeb Magruder, and John Dean on charges of conspiracy to obstruct justice. Donald Segretti had pleaded guilty to charges of conspiracy and distributing campaign literature without properly identifying its source, in connection with his "dirty tricks" operation. Egil Krogh, Jr had been indicted for lying to the grand jury in prior testimony regarding the "Plumbers" activities. Three large corporations—American Airlines, Goodyear Tire and Rubber, and Minnesota Mining and Manufacturing—had entered guilty pleas to making illegal corporate contributions in the 1972 Presidential election, as had the responsible officers of two of them. Dwayne Andreas and his First Interoceanic Corporation had been charged with the same offenses. Other investigations had progressed, and were expected to produce additional indictments and guilty pleas. In the negotiations leading to their guilty pleas, Segretti, LaRue, Magruder, and Dean had agreed to disclose to WSPF what they knew about the Watergate case and other matters under investigation.

Dean's guilty plea and agreement to cooperate with the prosecutors came October 19, the last day for the President to seek Supreme Court review of the decision ordering him to produce the tapes. Instead of asking the Supreme Court to hear the case, he announced a proposed compromise: Senator John Stennis would listen to the tapes and review a statement of their contents; if verified by Stennis the statement would then be given to the Special Prosecutor and the grand jury. Under an integral part of the proposal, Cox would agree not to litigate further with respect to the nine tapes or to seek additional tapes in the future.

In a news conference the following day, Cox stated his reasons for not accepting the proposal. Edited summaries, he noted, probably would not be admissible as evidence in court. His agreement not to seek additional tapes would prevent WSPF from conducting its investigations thoroughly. And the order to accept the compromise terms, he said, was inconsistent with the pledge of independence he had received from Attorney General Richardson at the time of his appointment.

That evening, October 20, the White House announced the events that came to be known as the "Saturday Night Massacre": President Nixon ordered Attorney General Richardson to dismiss Cox for his refusal to accept the White House proposal; Richardson resigned rather than carry out the order, and Deputy Attorney General William Ruckelshaus was fired for his refusal to obey; finally, Solicitor General Robert Bork, next in seniority at the Justice Department, dismissed Cox as Special Prosecutor. Also on White House orders, agents of the FBI occupied the offices of WSPF, the Attorney General, and the Deputy Attorney General in order to prevent the removal of any documents. WSPF staff members, gathered in their offices, were informed that they would work henceforth as part of the Justice Department's Criminal Division.

The events leading to Cox's dismissal had been foreshadowed by a number of his contacts with Attorney General Richardson over the previous months. On several occasions Richardson had asked whether particular matters Cox appeared to be investigating were under his jurisdiction and had expressed concern that Cox's inquiries were going into areas not contemplated when WSPF was established. Some of these questions were inherent in the apparent breadth of Cox's charter. Other questions arose from Richardson's own misgivings, and those of White House officials.

The actions which Richardson raised in conversation with Cox included WSPF's possible inquiry into the financing of President Nixon's two homes, its broad letters to several Federal agencies asking their policies and practices in electronic surveillance, the interviewing of a former White House aide who had prepared a controversial plan for intelligence gathering by the executive branch, investigation of wiretaps claimed to be justified by national security, and an inquiry into the handling of campaign contributions by a close friend of the President. In July, because both he and Cox were uneasy about the prospect of a series of politically motivated referrals to WSPF of charges against the President or his Administration, with attendant publicity, Richardson had suggested that the Criminal Division screen all allegations to determine whether they were substantial and fell within WSPF's jurisdiction before sending them on to Cox. Cox quickly rejected this proposal and Richardson did not pursue it. In August, citing the concerns of White House officials that Cox was reaching beyond his charter, Richardson proposed revising the Special Prosecutor's charter to define his jurisdiction with more precise limitations, and appointing a special consultant on national security matters to serve as an expediting intermediary between the Special Prosecutor and agencies from which he was seeking information regarding such matters. Cox felt that it was his own responsibility to determine what matters fell within the terms of his existing charter, and rejected any charter revisions as unnecessary. Cox also disagreed with the idea of a national security consultant because he saw such an official as a possible hindrance rather than an aid to obtaining necessary information.

Richardson also informed Cox of White House positions on various issues, including the production of evidence in response to the Special Prosecutor's requests. Despite their willingness to take independent positions on such legal issues as executive privilege and national security,

Richardson and Cox had also made efforts to reach agreement on such issues. During the period just before his resignation and Cox's dismissal, Richardson had made efforts to achieve a compromise on the question of the Special Prosecutor's access to the subpoenaed tapes.

OCTOBER 20, 1973–AUGUST 9, 1974

The "Saturday Night Massacre" did not halt the work of WSPF, and the prosecutors resumed their grand jury sessions as scheduled the following Tuesday. Bork placed Assistant Attorney General Henry Petersen, head of the Criminal Division, in charge of the investigations WSPF had been conducting. Both men assured the staff that its work would continue with the cooperation of the Justice Department and without interference from the White House. Upon WSPF's request, Judge Sirica issued a protective order to limit access to, and prevent removal of, WSPF files. Despite their anger over Cox's dismissal and their doubts about the future of their office, the staff members, in a series of meetings, decided to continue their work for the time being.

Nevertheless, the dismissal of Cox and the President's refusal to produce the subpoenaed tapes provoked what one White House official called a "firestorm" of public criticism and serious talk of impeachment on Capitol Hill. In an abrupt reversal, the President announced on October 23 that he would comply with the grand jury subpoena and on October 26 that Bork would appoint a new Special Prosecutor who would have "total cooperation from the executive branch." While the President said he would be unwilling to produce additional White House tapes or other evidence that he considered privileged, he placed no restrictions on the new Special Prosecutor's authority to seek such evidence through the courts.

On November 1, the President announced that he would nominate Senator William B. Saxbe as the new Attorney General. Later that day, Acting Attorney General Bork announced his appointment of Leon Jaworski as Special Prosecutor. Jaworski, who was sworn into office November 5, was assured the same jurisdiction and guarantees of independence as Cox, with the additional provision that he could be dismissed, or his jurisdiction limited, only with consent of a bipartisan group of eight Congressional leaders. Three days after taking office, Jaworski told a House subcommittee that the continuity of WSPF operations had been restored and that the office's staff would remain intact.

Meanwhile, a number of bills had been introduced in Congress to provide for judicial appointment or other safeguards of the independence of the Special Prosecutor. In the wake of the "Saturday Night Massacre," many people thought it impossible to assure an independent investigation by anyone appointed solely by the executive branch of Government or subject to dismissal without Congressional approval. Others including Chief Judge Sirica and some of his fellow judges opposed the idea of a court-appointed prosecutor, and Saxbe testified that he had accepted his nomination only on the condition that Jaworski's investigation would remain independent. Jaworski testified that he would welcome any legislation protecting his independence further, but was satisfied with his charter and the assurances he had been given. In mid-November, ruling on a civil suit that challenged the dismissal of Cox, District Judge Gerhard Gesell held that Cox's firing had been illegal. However, noting that Cox had not sought reinstatement, the judge said there was no reason to interfere with Jaworski's tenure. As a result of all these events, Congress abandoned the idea of establishing a Special Prosecutor's office by legislation.

Less than a week after the President's attorney had told Judge Sirica that the nine subpoenaed tapes would be produced for his examination, another White House lawyer announced that two of the conversations for which tapes had been sought had in fact never been recorded. Shortly thereafter, during a court inquiry into the question of the President's compliance with the subpoena, White House lawyers disclosed that the tape of a third conversation contained a substantial "gap"—a humming sound which obliterated some 18½ minutes of one of the President's conversations—and that dictabelts of the President's recollections of two of the conversations contained shorter gaps. A panel of experts chosen by White House and WSPF lawyers reported in January 1974 that the 18½-minute gap had been caused by a series of deliberate erasures, and that it was impossible to retrieve the original conversation. Judge Sirica thereupon referred the matter to a grand jury. A lengthy investigation, conducted by WSPF and the FBI, concluded that only a small number of people had had the opportunity to make the erasures but was unable to fix criminal responsibility on any particular individual or individuals.

Meanwhile, the task force investigations continued. By the end of 1973, five more corporations—Braniff Airways, Ashland Petroleum Gabon Inc., Gulf Oil Corporation, Phillips Petroleum Company, and Carnation Company—and their responsible officers—had pleaded guilty to making corporate contributions to 1972 Presidential campaigns. Former Presidential aide Dwight Chapin had been indicted for making false statements to the grand jury in connection with Segretti's activities. Egil Krogh, Jr, former head of the White House "Plumbers," had entered a guilty plea to conspiring to violate the rights of Dr Fielding, whose office had been broken into in a vain attempt to obtain Daniel Ellsberg's psychiatric records.

The new year brought additional indictments and guilty pleas. Herbert Porter, a former aide in the President's re-election campaign, pleaded guilty to making false statements in connection with the original investigation of the Watergate case. Jake Jacobsen, an attorney who had helped milk producer cooperatives make campaign contributions and obtain an increase in milk price supports, was indicted on charges of making false statements to the grand jury. Herbert Kalmbach, the President's personal lawyer and an active campaign fundraiser, pleaded guilty to a felony violation of the Federal Corrupt Practices Act in his fundraising for candidates in the 1970 Congressional elections and to a charge of promising an ambassadorship to a campaign contributor.

Efforts to obtain additional recordings and other documents from the White House, for use as evidence in various grand jury investigations, continued during the winter of 1973–74. For a short period after Jaworski took office, the White House offered limited cooperation by supplying some of the numerous tapes and documents requested by WSPF over the past four months. In January, however, the President retained as counsel James St Clair, whose major concern appeared to be protecting him against possible impeachment. The President stopped his initial cooperation with Jaworski, and WSPF requests were soon met by unusual delays and claims that some materials could not be located. Other materials, the President said, were unnecessary to the grand jury investigations. To furnish them would be inconsistent with his constitutional responsibilities.

During the winter, and again in the late spring of 1974, Jaworski met periodically with General Alexander Haig, the President's chief of staff. For the most part, these meetings involved attempts by Jaworski to persuade Haig that the President should provide WSPF with materials it was seeking. Haig complained about particular actions by WSPF staff members, including their intensive questioning of White House witnesses in the grand jury and their efforts to have FBI agents interview White House staff members in connection with the investigation of the 18½-minute tape gap.

On March 1, the grand jury returned an indictment in the Watergate cover-up case of seven men formerly associated with the White House or CRP—Charles Colson, John Ehrlichman, H. R. Haldeman, Robert Mardian, John Mitchell, Kenneth Parkinson, and Gordon Strachan—on charges of conspiracy, obstruction of justice, and, as of some, perjury and false declarations. A week later six men—Bernard Barker, Colson, Felipe DeDiego, Ehrlichman, Gordon Liddy, and Eugenio Martinez—were indicted for conspiring to violate Dr Fielding's civil rights in connection with the illegal entry of his office, and Ehrlichman was charged in addition with making false statements to the FBI and the grand jury about the case.

The grand jury hearing evidence in the Watergate case concluded that President Nixon had been a participant in the cover-up. However, after extensive legal research in the office, Jaworski concluded that it would be improper to indict an incumbent President for such a crime when the House of Representatives' Judiciary Committee had already begun a formal impeachment inquiry. He believed, in addition, that such an indictment would be challenged and ultimately overturned by the Supreme Court, and that the fruitless litigation would delay the trial of the seven cover-up defendants and possibly also temporarily halt the impeachment inquiry. The grand jury then authorized the Special Prosecutor to name President Nixon as an unindicted co-conspirator in the cover-up case. Since this finding was relevant to the impeachment investigation, WSPF asked the grand jury to report to the court all of its evidence relating to the President's alleged involvement in the cover-up, with a recommendation that Judge Sirica forward the report to the House Judiciary Committee. The grand jury did so and by order of Judge Sirica, upheld by the Court of Appeals, the report was delivered to the Committee on March 26.

Discussions had been held between Committee Attorneys and WSPF several months before. The prosecutors felt obligated to assist the Committee to the extent that such assistance was legally proper and would not jeopardize WSPF's investigations. In February, with the consent of White House counsel, WSPF had provided the Committee with a list of tapes and documents it had received from the White House, and in March the office supplied a list of those items requested from White House files but not received. As soon as the existence of the grand jury report became public knowledge, the President's counsel agreed to supply the Committee with all materials that had been supplied to the Special Prosecutor, and he subsequently did so. Later in the spring, when the Committee sought access to various records under seal of the court, the Special Prosecutor on most occasions indicated his approval. WSPF's task force heads also met on several occasions with Committee Attorneys to provide relevant information. Necessary ground rules protected the secrecy of grand jury proceedings and the confidentiality of WSPF sources of information. The prosecutors suggested what witnesses the Committee should interview on what subjects, and what lines of inquiry were likely to prove fruitless for their purposes.

After months of frustrating efforts to obtain grand jury and trial evidence from the White House, including recordings of Presidential conversations, Jaworski decided that he would have to resort, as his predecessor had, to judicial process. A grand jury subpoena of March 15 had resulted in the production of campaign contribution documents from White House files but had not called for Presidential tapes. At Jaworski's request, Judge Sirica issued a trial subpoena on April 18 in the cover-up case for recordings and documents related to 64 specified Presidential conversations. Unlike the previous subpoenas, which had been issued by the grand juries in connection with their investigations, this one was issued by the court so that WSPF could prepare adequately for the trial in the Watergate case, then scheduled to begin early in September.

On April 30, two days before the date for compliance with the trial subpoena, the President released to the public edited transcripts of some of the recorded conversations which had been subpoenaed by both the House Committee and WSPF, claiming that "the materials ... will tell it all." The next day, he formally refused to provide the tapes to Judge Sirica contending that some of the materials covered by the subpoena were protected by executive privilege, that disclosure would be "contrary to the public interest," and that the subpoena was invalid because the tapes would be inadmissible as evidence. His attorneys filed a motion to quash the subpoena.

Jaworski informed Haig and St Clair a few days later that imminent argument in court by WSPF in an effort to enforce the subpoena would require the statement that the President had been named as an unindicted co-conspirator. Jaworski offered to withdraw the subpoena, thus postponing disclosure of the President's status until later trial proceedings, if the White House supplied voluntarily 16 specified tape recordings that WSPF considered crucial. A few days later, after listening to the tapes in question, the President sent word to Jaworski that his proposed compromise was unacceptable.

During ensuing litigation over the White House motion to quash the subpoena, the President's counsel asserted that the Special Prosecutor, as an employee of the executive branch, lacked authority to seek evidence from the White House by judicial process. This renewed the argument used seven months earlier to justify the dismissal of Cox. In accordance with a promise he had made when appointed, Jaworski immediately informed the chairman of the Senate Judiciary Committee and House Judiciary Committee of the new challenge to his independence. By resolution the following day, the Senate Committee affirmed its support of Jaworski's right to take the President to court, and urged Attorney General Saxbe to "use all reasonable and appropriate means to guarantee the independence" of the Special Prosecutor. Two days later, Saxbe promised the Committee that he would support WSPF's independence.

On May 20, Judge Sirica denied the President's motion to quash and ordered him to comply with the subpoena. After the President's lawyers announced their decision to appeal this order, Jaworski asked the Supreme Court to consider the matter as soon as possible, bypassing the Court of Appeals in order to avoid unnecessary delays. The Supreme Court agreed to do so, over White House opposition.

After legal briefs and oral arguments had been scheduled in an unusual summer session, the Court ruled unanimously on July 24 that the President must comply with the subpoena. While recognizing for the first time the Constitutional doctrine of executive privilege, the Court held that "the generalized assertion of privilege must yield to the demonstrated specific need for evidence in a pending criminal trial." The President announced that he would comply with the Court's ruling and with the subpoena.

In the days that followed, the House Judiciary Committee concluded its inquiry by adopting three articles of impeachment to be reported to the full House of Representatives for its consideration.

On August 5, the President released to the public transcripts of portions of recorded conversations held six days after the Watergate break-in. His accompanying statement acknowledged that in the conversations he had ordered steps taken to conceal from the FBI the involvement of White House and campaign officials, and he admitted that he had kept this evidence from his own lawyers and Congressional supporters. On August 9, in the face of overwhelming support for impeachment in the House and almost certain conviction in the Senate, he resigned the Presidency.

The Special Prosecutor's efforts to obtain Watergate trial evidence from President Nixon did not inhibit other WSPF investigations and prosecutions. A trial jury convicted Dwight Chapin of lying about his knowledge of campaign "dirty tricks." Gordon Liddy, one of the men convicted in the original Watergate break-in case, was indicted, tried, and convicted of contempt of Congress, for his refusal to testify before a House Committee. The ITT investigations resulted in two convictions: former Attorney General Richard Kleindienst pleaded guilty to giving inaccurate testimony to a Senate Committee, and Lieutenant Governor Ed Reinecke of California, who chose to stand trial, was convicted of perjury.

Investigations of campaign contribution activity also continued during the spring and summer of 1974. Diamond International Corporation, Northrop Corporation, Lehigh Valley Cooperative Farmers, and National By-Products, Inc., all entered guilty pleas to making illegal campaign contributions. The principal officer of Diamond, two officers of Lehigh Valley, and two officers of Northrop pleaded guilty to similar charges. American Ship Building Company and its chairman George Steinbrenner were indicted for making illegal contributions, and Steinbrenner was also charged with conspiracy and obstruction of the grand jury's inquiry. Another official of American Ship Building acknowledged guilt as an accessory to an illegal contribution. A jury in New York found John Mitchell and Maurice Stans, two former members of President Nixon's cabinet, not guilty of charges connected with contributions by financier Robert Vesco, and a federal judge in Minnesota acquitted the First Interoceanic Corporation and Dwayne Andreas of illegal contribution charges.

The investigation into the campaign activities of Associated Milk Producers, Inc. (AMPI) resulted in several prosecutions. Former AMPI officials Harold Nelson and David Parr pleaded guilty to conspiracy charges, with Nelson also acknowledging his part in a conspiracy to make an illegal payment to a public official. AMPI entered a guilty plea to charges of conspiracy and making five corporate contributions. The perjury charge against attorney Jake Jacobsen had been dismissed on technical grounds, but he pleaded guilty to a later charge of making illegal payments to a public official. The same indictment charged former Treasury Secretary John Connally with accepting such payments and with conspiracy and perjury. Later in the summer of 1974, Norman Sherman and John Valentine pleaded guilty to aiding and abetting unlawful AMPI contributions.

While WSPF's subpoena of White House tapes for the Watergate trial was pending before Judge Sirica, Judge Gerhard Gesell was hearing pretrial motions in the Fielding break-in case. Because of doubts about the legal effect of a previous grant of immunity to defendant Felipe DeDiego, the judge dismissed the charges against him. Judge Gesell also ruled against a defense argument that the entry into Dr Fielding's office had been justified by considerations of national security. Shortly after this ruling, one of the defendants, former White House aide Charles Colson, pleaded guilty to obstructing justice in the federal criminal case brought against Daniel Ellsberg after his public release of the "Pentagon Papers." Colson admitted that White House efforts to discredit Ellsberg by public release of derogatory information were intended to interfere with his fair trial. As a result of this plea and his agreement to disclose what he knew about matters under the Special Prosecutor's jurisdiction, the charges against Colson in the Watergate case and the original charges against him in the Fielding break-in case were dropped. The break-in trial began June 26, and ended July 12, with the convictions of the four remaining defendants—Bernard Barker, John Ehrlichman, Gordon Liddy, and Eugenio Martinez.

AUGUST 9, 1974–OCTOBER 1, 1975

The Nixon resignation presented WSPF with an immediate question: should the former President be prosecuted as a private citizen for whatever crimes he might have committed while in office? Jaworski, after announcing that he had reached no agreement or understanding with anyone about the former President's possible prosecution, said he intended to defer a decision on whether to seek any indictments. The WSPF staff needed time to analyze all the relevant factors. But, on September 8, before the Special Prosecutor had decided whether to seek an indictment, President Ford pardoned his predecessor for any and all Federal crimes he might have committed while President.

President Nixon's resignation also raised questions of access to the White House papers and recordings which WSPF needed in its investigations of possible criminal conduct during his Administration. President Ford's counsel told WSPF on August 15, that the former President's files would be kept in White House custody until their ownership had been resolved. However, when he announced the pardon September 8, President Ford also revealed an agreement—made without any prior notice to the Special Prosecutor—giving the former President control over access to the files, which would be kept in a Government installation near the Nixon residence in California. President Ford based his position on a Justice Department opinion that the former President was the legal owner of the materials, and on his belief that their physical security could be assured by maintaining them in Government custody. The Special Prosecutor disagreed with the President's view of the situation and suggested that he might challenge the September 8 agreement in court. Resulting discussions among WSPF, Justice Department, and White House officials produced an agreement whereby the Nixon files would remain in White House custody pending review of the question of WSPF's access to them.

On October 17, the former President filed a lawsuit to compel enforcement of the September 8 agreement giving him control over access to his White House files. The court issued a temporary restraining order prohibiting access to the materials without the consent of attorneys for both the former President and President Ford. On November 9, based on President Ford's determination that the needs of justice required direct access to the Nixon files by the Special Prosecutor's office, the President's counsel, along with the directors of the General Services Administration and the Secret Service, agreed in writing with the Special Prosecutor on procedures for direct access by WSPF. The Special Prosecutor' office then began discussions with former President Nixon's counsel to obtain his consent to this agreement.

Because of the needs of all parties to prepare adequately for trial, the Watergate cover-up trial was postponed from September 9 to October 1, pursuant to a suggestion from the Court of Appeals to Judge Sirica. Doubts about the effect on the prosecution's case of grants of immunity to defendant Gordon Strachan led to his severance from the trial.[5] On October 12, shortly after the jury had been sequestered, Special Prosecutor Jaworski announced that he would resign as of October 26, stating that the bulk of the office's work had been completed. He also announced that he had decided not to challenge President Ford's pardon of former President Nixon in the courts because he did not believe such a challenge would have any chance of prevailing. Thus WSPF ended its consideration of the former President as a possible defendant. Jaworski was succeeded October 26 by Henry S. Ruth, Jr, who had served as deputy to both of the previous Special Prosecutors.

During the months following President Nixon's resignation, WSPF obtained additional indictments and convictions. George Steinbrenner and the American Ship Building Company pleaded guilty to charges of conspiracy and making an illegal campaign contribution, and "DKI for '74," a committee supporting the re-election of Senator Daniel Inouye, pleaded guilty to failing to report a contribution received from Steinbrenner. Guilty pleas for illegal contributions were entered by LBC&W, Inc., and its principal officer, Greyhound Corporation, Ashland Oil, Inc., Ratrie, Robbins, and Schweitzer, Inc., and its principal officers, and the principal officer of HMS Electric Corporation. Tim Babcock, an executive of Occidental Petroleum Corp., and formerly Governor of Montana,

---

5. Charges against Strachan were dismissed on the Special Prosecutor's motion March 10, 1975.

pleaded guilty to making a campaign contribution in another person's name. Oklahoma lawyer Stuart Russell and Minnesota lawyer Jack Chestnut were both indicted in connection with milk-producer contribution activities. Jack Gleason and Harry Dent, former White House aides, pleaded guilty to violating the Federal Corrupt Practices Act in their fundraising for the 1970 Congressional elections. Edward Morgan, a former Deputy Counsel in the White House, pleaded guilty to conspiracy to defraud the Government in connection with an income tax deduction taken by former President Nixon.

Most of these actions occurred as the Watergate cover-up trial was taking place during the autumn of 1974 in Judge Sirica's courtroom. Efforts to obtain former President Nixon's testimony at the trial were frustrated when three court-appointed physicians reported that his serious illness prevented his testimony for several months. After a three-month trial, defendants Ehrlichman, Haldeman, Mardian and Mitchell were found guilty by the jury, and defendant Parkinson was acquitted.

Early in 1975, WSPF's staff began a steady reduction as investigations and prosecutions were completed, but office business continued through the spring and summer. Los Angeles lawyer Frank DeMarco and Chicago book dealer and appraiser Ralph Newman were indicted on conspiracy and other charges related to their roles in the preparation of former President Nixon's income tax returns. Former Secretary of Commerce Maurice Stans, who had headed the Finance Committee to Re-Elect the President, pleaded guilty to three violations of the Federal Election Campaign Act's reporting requirements and to two violations of accepting corporate contributions. Former Treasury Secretary Connally was found not guilty by a jury on charges of accepting illegal payments, and the remaining charges against him were dismissed. A New York City jury convicted Jack Chestnut of a felony for aiding and abetting an illegal milk-producer contribution[6] and a San Antonio, Texas, jury convicted Stuart Russell of three felonies for conspiracy and aiding and abetting other dairy industry contributions. Former Congressman Wendell Wyatt pleaded guilty to a reporting violation under the Federal Election Campaign Act.

Discussions with the former President's counsel about WSPF access to Nixon Administration tapes and documents resulted in an understanding that permitted the prosecutors to obtain relevant evidence. Beginning in February 1975, with an index prepared by Government archivists, the prosecutors designated the particular files they wanted searched for documents and recordings related to specified investigations. The file searches were conducted by archivists under the supervision of President Ford's counsel; former President Nixon's attorney reviewed all requested recordings of Presidential conversations and provided copies of those which might be pertinent to WSPF's investigations. Between February and June, WSPF obtained numerous documents and tapes generated in the White House during the Nixon Administration. On June 23 and 24, after negotiations with the former President's counsel, several WSPF attorneys and two members of the grand jury took Nixon's testimony under oath near his California residence.

A considerable portion of the prosecutor's work in 1975 involved the numerous appeals that followed convictions at trial and other court actions. Matters on appeal included the convictions in the 1973 Watergate trial, the later Watergate cover-up trial, the Fielding break-in, the

---

6. After the WSPF investigation and grand jury indictment, the office of the United States Attorney for the Southern District of New York conducted the trial at WSPF's request.

trials of Dwight Chapin, Ed Reinecke, and Stuart Russell, and the sentence imposed on Tim Babcock. The prosecutors unsuccessfully sought reversal of a court order moving the trials of Frank DeMarco and Ralph Newman to two separate cities and intervened in litigation to oppose Mr Nixon's contention that the Presidential Recordings and Materials Preservation Act of 1974 deprived him unconstitutionally of his Presidential papers. The appellate process in some cases is expected to extend at least through 1976.

The grand juries which had heard evidence obtained by WSPF were dismissed when their terms expired. The first, originally empaneled on June 5, 1972, and extended by legislation, was dismissed on December 4, 1974. After having sat for the standard 18-month term, the second was dismissed February 12, 1975, and the third, July 3, 1975.

MAJOR INVESTIGATIONS AND OTHER ACTIONS

The five task forces of WSPF conducted investigations of several hundred separate matters, and the counsel's office provided legal and policy advice and other services to the task forces and the Special Prosecutor. The most important work of the five task forces and the counsel's office is described in summary form in this chapter. Not included are large numbers of investigations each of which involved a relatively minor commitment of office resources and did not result in criminal charges. Also omitted are a number of investigations requiring substantial efforts which have not been publicly disclosed in the past and which did not result in charges. Reporting them here would publicize, for the first time and in an improper forum, allegations from which the prosecutors concluded they should not initiate court action for various reasons. In the investigations included within this chapter, allegations are cited if they have already received extensive publicity or if they had become public through court proceedings, legislative inquiries or other forums. As to these also, when no prosecution resulted, the prosecutors made the decision on the basis of established practice of the WSPF.

WATERGATE TASK FORCE

Investigation of Watergate cover-up

When WSPF was established in May 1973, seven men already had been convicted of burglary, conspiracy, and wiretapping charges in connection with the break-in at the Democratic National Committee headquarters on June 17, 1972. Part of the public testimony before the Senate Select Committee supported allegations that high officials of the Administration and the President's re-election campaign either had sponsored the break-in or had tried to prevent the original investigation from reaching beyond those seven. In addition, the Assistant US Attorneys for the District of Columbia, who had handled the investigation until the Special Prosecutor's appointment, had obtained information strongly suggesting the involvement of others.

By October 19, as a result of information developed by the US Attorney's office and then by WSPF, three important witnesses had pleaded guilty to conspiracy charges in connection with the cover-up—former campaign officials Fred LaRue and Jeb Magruder and former White House counsel John Dean. All three later testified for the prosecution at the trial of others involved. WSPF also obtained a guilty plea from former campaign official Herbert Porter, to a charge of making false statements to a Government agency in connection with the cover-up.

Along with efforts in the summer and fall of 1973 to obtain the cooperation of these witnesses, WSPF also attempted to obtain by grand jury subpoena other relevant evidence in the form of documents and tape recordings of Presidential conversations. Special Prosecutor Cox's efforts to obtain compliance with the subpoena resulted in his dismissal at President Nixon's direction in October, followed by the appointment of Special Prosecutor Jaworski and the production of some of the subpoenaed materials. The President's compliance with the subpoena was incomplete, however (see below, the discussion of the 18½-minute gap), and the necessary inquiries into the causes of his failure to so comply further delayed the development and presentation to the grand jury of evidence relating to the cover-up.

Nevertheless, by March 1974, the grand jury had obtained sufficient evidence to hand up indictments on charges of conspiracy, obstruction of justice and perjury; seven men formerly associated with the White House or the President's campaign committee were named as defendants to one or more of the charges—Charles Colson, John Ehrlichman, H. R. Haldeman, Robert Mardian, John Mitchell, Kenneth Parkinson, and Gordon Strachan. At the Special Prosecutor's suggestion, the grand jury also submitted a report which the court transmitted under seal to the House Judiciary Committee in connection with its inquiry into the possible impeachment of President Nixon. The report contained evidence relevant to the Committee's inquiry into the President's possible involvement in the cover-up. In addition, the grand jury authorized the Special Prosecutor to name 18 individuals, including President Nixon, as unindicted co-conspirators.

After the indictment, the Special Prosecutor obtained a trial subpoena for additional White House tapes and documents. Much of the summer of 1974 was consumed by litigation over the validity of this subpoena, which was eventually upheld by the Supreme Court, and by examination of the materials produced in compliance with the court's decision. During this period, the House Committee completed its impeachment inquiry by recommending the President's impeachment, the President publicly released transcripts of several subpoena tapes which showed him to have been a participant in the cover-up, and he resigned his office August 9. The prosecutors immediately began to review the question of his possible criminal liability, but before any final decision could be made on whether to recommend his indictment he was pardoned by his successor, President Ford.

By the time the trial started on October 1, charges against Colson had been dismissed as a result of his guilty plea in another case (see below, the discussion of Fielding break-in), and those against Strachan had been severed. The trial of the five remaining defendants, which lasted three months, resulted in the convictions of Ehrlichman, Haldeman, Mardian, and Mitchell, and the acquittal of Parkinson. Mitchell, Haldeman and Ehrlichman were each sentenced to serve 2½ to 8 years imprisonment, while Mardian received a 10-month to 3-year prison sentence. All four convictions are now on appeal. The charges against Strachan were dismissed on motion of the Special Prosecutor because the legal effect of immunity granted to him by the Assistant US Attorneys and the Senate Committee created doubts about whether he could be tried without infringing upon his constitutional privilege against self-incrimination.

After the Watergate cover-up trial, intensive investigation and consideration was devoted to possible perjury and obstruction of justice by two other persons during the course of the 1972–73 cover-up investigation. Evidentiary and legal problems prevented initiation of prosecution in these matters.

Investigation of 18½-minute tape gap

On October 23, 1973, the White House agreed to provide the US District Court for the District of Columbia with subpoenaed tapes, notes, and memoranda of nine Presidential conversations related to the Watergate cover-up. Seven conversations were produced, but White House counsel claimed that the remaining two had not been recorded. This assertion led Judge Sirica to hold hearings beginning October 31 to determine the facts. On November 21, while the hearings were recessed to await further testimony on the failure to record the two conversations, White House counsel Fred Buzhardt requested an in-chambers meeting with Chief Judge John Sirica and attorneys from WSPF. At that meeting, Buzhardt announced that the subpoenaed tape of a conversation between President Nixon and H. R. Haldeman on June 20, 1972—three days after the Watergate break-in—had been obliterated inexplicably by a buzzing sound lasting 18½ minutes. Haldeman's notes of that meeting indicated that the obliterated portion of the tape covered only that part of the conversation which was related to the break-in.

The discovery of this tape gap led Judge Sirica to reopen the hearings, which continued for seven days in late November and early December. The President's secretary, Rose Mary Woods, testified at the public hearing that she might have accidentally erased four or five minutes of the subpoenaed tape on October 1, 1973, while transcribing the conversation. She explained that this possible erasure occurred when she inadvertently left her foot on the pedal controlling the tape recorder while answering the telephone and conducting a conversation. In addition to Miss Woods' testimony, other White House aides, attorneys, and Secret Service personnel answered questions about the storage of the tape, the methods used to transcribe it, who had access to it, and the discovery of the gap. Testimony and access logs kept by custodians of the tapes revealed that, after being recorded, this tape had been routinely placed in a storage vault and not disturbed until September 28, 1973, two months after it had been subpoenaed by the grand jury. Any mishandling of the tape appeared to have occurred between that date and the discovery of the gap by White House counsel on November 14, 1973.

In a further effort to ascertain the cause of the 18½-minute gap, the court appointed a panel of six experts in acoustics and sound engineering approved by the White House and WSPF. The panel was asked to determine the method by which the gap had been created, the kind of machine that had been used to create it, and the existence of any possibility of recovering the conversation. The experts began various tests on the tape early in December in the presence of representatives of the White House and WSPF. Their report, delivered to the court January 15, 1974, concluded that the gap had been produced by at least five separate hand operations of the stop and record buttons of a Uher 5000 machine, the same model used by Woods in transcribing the tape. The panel also concluded that recovery of the obliterated conversation would be impossible.

Since the experts' report made it clear that the gap had been caused by intentional erasures, and evidence produced at the hearings showed that the erasures had occurred after the tape had been subpoenaed, Judge Sirica referred the matter to the grand jury for further investigation of the possibility of obstruction of justice. A grand jury, assisted by WSPF and the FBI, began hearing witnesses January 28, 1974. It concluded from the testimony of over 50 people that a very small number of persons could have been responsible for the erasures, but it was unable to obtain evidence sufficient to prosecute any individual.

Investigation of submission of Presidential transcripts to House Judiciary Committee[1]

On April 30, 1974, President Nixon authorized the submission to the House Judiciary Committee, and the release to the public, of a number of transcripts of recorded conversations. The Committee had subpoenaed the original of these conversations in connection with its impeachment inquiry. At the same time, the President offered to allow the Committee's chairman and ranking minority member to listen to the original tapes and verify the accuracy and completeness of the transcripts. The Committee declined this offer.

The Committee and WSPF had already obtained some of the tapes of conversations included in the transcripts, and comparison of the WSPF transcripts with the White House transcripts showed that the latter contained several omissions of portions of conversations. The prosecutors made some inquiries in the months following the transcripts' release, but investigation had to await WSPF's receipt of additional tapes in August 1974, pursuant to the trial subpoena in the Watergate cover-up case. A full-scale investigation began early in 1975 to determine whether various materials were deleted from the transcripts for the purpose of obstructing the Judiciary Committee's inquiry in violation of Title 18, United States Code, Section 1505. To establish a violation of this section it would be necessary to prove that portions of the conversations damaging to the President were willfully deleted with the corrupt intent to mislead the Committee.

Certain problems made the necessary elements difficult to prove. The Committee already possessed the tapes of

---

1. Although this matter arose as part of the Watergate cover-up investigation, the inquiry detailed in this section was conducted by attorneys not assigned to the Watergate task force.

several of these conversations, and as to these, White House deletions in transcripts could not mislead or obstruct the Committee. The WSPF investigation thus excluded those transcripts from consideration. Further, President Nixon submitted his transcripts with the express statement that he was providing only the information that he felt was necessary to Committee business. More significantly, however, in view of the White House offer to allow Committee representatives to listen to the tapes for their own verification, corrupt intent was difficult, if not impossible, to establish unless direct proof existed either to negate the bona fides of this Presidential offer to the Committee, or to show an explicitly stated intention to deceive. Finally, the White House transcripts carefully noted that deleted material was "not related to Presidential *action*" (emphasis supplied). The choice of this language to characterize the deletions introduced great ambiguity in the intent factor; an advocate could state with literal truth that the Committee was put on notice by this language that Watergate-related conversations may have been omitted from the transcripts when the conversation had not been followed by specific actions.

This investigation was conducted in large part through the interviewing of various witnesses by WSPF and the FBI, outside of the grand jury. The investigation began with a comparison of WSPF transcripts with those prepared by the White House. Seven or eight deletions were selected which, because of their length and nature, could not realistically have been omitted because of a problem in audibly determining what was on the tape. WSPF focused the investigation on these deletions and attempted to determine why they took place. Almost all persons involved in the preparation of the transcripts in the White House were interviewed to track the transcription process and the course of decision-making as to the deletions. These and other persons were also interviewed in order to check the bona fides of the Presidential offer to have Committee representatives listen to the entire tape for omissions they thought might be relevant to the Committee impeachment inquiry.

WSPF concluded that there is strong circumstantial evidence that at least some of the lengthy deletions were deliberate, but no prosecution was possible. No direct evidence existed to overcome the above problems of establishing the necessary criminal intent. In addition, all the available evidence indicated that the verification offer by the White House to the Committee was made with full expectations that the offer might indeed be accepted.

"DIRTY TRICKS" INVESTIGATION

In October 1973, several newspapers reported that President Nixon's re-election campaign included an under-cover network of agents who had engaged in various kinds of political espionage and sabotage against candidates for the Democratic Presidential nomination. The reported activities came to be known collectively as "dirty tricks," and included forging letters and other literature which unfairly attacked some candidates, planting manufactured stories in the press, copying documents from campaign files, and recruiting people to ask embarrassing questions at candidates' rallies or to picket such rallies on behalf of opposing candidates. The *Washington Post* identified California lawyer Donald Segretti as the director of these operations and reported that he had been recruited and paid by White House staff members and re-election campaign aides.

The press disclosures, along with complaints by one of the Democratic candidates whose Florida primary campaign had been a target of such activities, led the US Attorney's office for the Middle District of Florida to conduct an investigation with the help of the FBI. Segretti and George A. Hearing, one of Segretti's associates, were indicted on May 4, 1973, in Florida on charges of conspiracy and distributing campaign literature without properly identifying its source. A week later, Hearing pleaded guilty and was sentenced to a year's imprisonment.

Even before Segretti's indictment in Florida, the Assistant US Attorneys conducting the Watergate investigation in Washington had interviewed and questioned before the grand jury several former White House and re-election campaign officials about his sponsorship. After the appointment of Special Prosecutor Cox, the "dirty tricks" investigation was taken over by WSPF. Facing the Florida charges and possible charges in other states, Segretti offered in July to cooperate with WSPF, and met with the prosecutors twice that summer, giving information that indicated that former White House aide Dwight Chapin had lied to the grand jury about his involvement in Segretti's activities. Segretti later pleaded guilty to three misdemeanor charges in Washington, D.C., and was sentenced to serve six months in prison.

The day after his guilty plea, Segretti testified before the grand jury under a grant of immunity. His testimony and other evidence resulted in Chapin's indictment on four perjury charges on November 29. On April 5, 1974, after trial, Chapin was convicted on two of those charges; one of the remaining charges was dismissed during the trial, and the jury acquitted him of the other. Sentenced to serve 10 to 30 months in prison, Chapin filed an appeal. On July 14, 1975, the Court of Appeals affirmed his conviction.

The Florida investigation had identified several people who had engaged in "dirty tricks" as agents of Segretti. Some had been immunized in order to provide the Florida prosecutors with information about Segretti's own conduct. WSPF's subsequent investigation, which involved his operations in several states besides Florida, identified about 25 people who had engaged in various activities on his instructions. Most of them had engaged in conduct that was not criminal—for example, supplying Segretti with local news clippings, asking embarrassing questions at candidates' public appearances, peacefully picketing events at which candidates were to appear, putting Segretti in touch with other possible agents. Those who had engaged in more serious conduct, such as distributing misattributed literature, were generally young people who had done so without knowing it was illegal. Because of their youth, the marginal and isolated nature of their criminality, if any, and their low level of influence in Segretti's operation, WSPF did not seek to prosecute these persons.

Other allegations, including those made in the press and in testimony before the Senate Select Committee, indicated that various other "dirty tricks" had been perpetrated against Democratic campaigns by people working on behalf of the President's re-election. WSPF investigated these allegations and found either that they did not involve criminal conduct or that the filing of criminal charges was not warranted by the facts uncovered.

The prosecutors also received allegations about possible "dirty tricks" by agents of Democratic candidates directed against President Nixon's campaign. Most of these involved the possible use of Democratic candidates' headquarters and facilities in organizing demonstrations that disrupted public appearances of the President or of persons campaigning on his behalf. The most substantial of these charges was that Senator George McGovern's Los Angeles campaign headquarters and telephone bank had been used in organizing a large demonstration at the Century Plaza Hotel when the President appeared there in September 1972. As to this and the other matters they investigated, the prosecutors did not obtain sufficient evidence to bring criminal charges.

INVESTIGATIONS RELATING TO INTERNATIONAL TELEPHONE AND TELEGRAPH CORPORATION

During the spring of 1972, while the Senate Judiciary Committee was considering the nomination of Richard Kleindienst to be Attorney General, press accounts suggested that the Department of Justice had settled three antitrust suits in 1971 against International Telephone and Telegraph Corporation (ITT), one of the Nation's largest conglomerates, in return for ITT's alleged offer to help finance the 1972 Republican National Convention. The Committee questioned Kleindienst, other Government officials, officers of ITT, and others with relevant knowledge about the matter, and then requested the Justice Department to investigate the possibility that perjury had been committed in its hearings.

After WSPF was established, Attorney General Richardson, who had succeeded Kleindienst, asked Special Prosecutor Cox to look into the possibility that perjury had been committed in the 1972 hearings (the Justice Department's investigation had made little progress in the preceding year), as well as the possible relationship between the antitrust settlements and ITT's pledges of support for the Republican convention. He also asked Cox to investigate an allegation, referred to the Justice Department by the Securities and Exchange Commission (SEC), that a Commission inquiry had been obstructed by ITT's failure to produce certain documents. An ITT task force was organized within WSPF to conduct these inquiries.

Later, in response to additional referrals from the Justice Department and information received from other sources, the ITT task force also investigated charges that:

- The Kleindienst confirmation hearings had been illegally obstructed;
- Crimes had been committed in connection with the transfer of documents relating to ITT from the SEC to the Justice Department at a time when a House Commerce Subcommittee was seeking such documents and in connection with subsequent Subcommittee hearings inquiring into the circumstances of the transfer;
- ITT had been granted a favorable tax ruling by the Internal Revenue Service as a result of improper influence or fraud;
- Improper influence had been applied to the Justice Department's handling of the antitrust suits against ITT, apart from the 1971 settlement;
- Improper influence had been used in securing the agreement of another corporation to merge with ITT and in obtaining necessary approvals of that merger;
- Perjury had been committed by various people before Congressional committees, the SEC, and the grand jury.

The investigation into ITT-related matters occupied several attorneys for approximately 18 months. Investigation of the antitrust cases involved an examination of the July 1971 settlements and improper attempts to influence these settlements. The cases involved Government challenges to ITT's proposed mergers with the Canteen Corporation (filed in April 1969), the Hartford Fire Insurance Company (filed on August 1, 1969), and the Grinnell Corporation (filed on August 1, 1969). While other events were also examined, the principal focus was on determining whether illegal influence was exercised:

(1) to prevent the filing of the Canteen case or cause the Government not to seek preliminary relief enjoining that merger;

(2) to convince the Government in the summer and fall of 1970 either to drop the cases entirely or accept a settlement involving no meaningful divestiture;

(3) to prevent or delay the filing of an appeal in the Grinnell case to the Supreme Court; and

(4) to cause the settlement of all three cases in July 1971.

In each of these instances the evidence accumulated by WSPF showed that ITT had gained access, directly or indirectly, to important Administration officials who in some instances took some action relating to these cases. In only one instance did the effort to secure high-level influence produce a provable impact on the handling of the cases. The further task, however, was to discover whether these attempts to influence the case were corrupt, such as a result of a bribe, or whether they were the product of an intensive though legal lobbying effort. Those whose conduct was examined in this connection included persons who sought the assistance of Administration officials, the officials who discussed these cases with people outside the Government, and those with high-level responsibility for the cases who dealt with Administration officials.

The investigation relating to the Kleindienst confirmation hearings focused on two areas: first and more significant was whether any witness at the hearings had committed perjury; second, whether the hearings were obstructed illegally. In the search for possible perjury, the investigators examined the testimony of every witness who testified about the ITT antitrust cases and the San Diego convention pledge.

The obstruction inquiry is more difficult to define. It was clear that the Judiciary Committee did not receive the complete "story" during its hearings and did not obtain substantial numbers of pertinent ITT and Government (White House and Justice Department) documents. The goal of WSPF was to discover why this took place and whether the facts involved illegal defiance of Committee process or acts sufficient to constitute a violation of the criminal obstruction laws.

In June 1972, the Securities and Exchange Commission filed a case against ITT and certain of its officers in which a consent judgment was entered. In September and October 1972, the SEC began to examine whether ITT had improperly withheld subpoenaed documents. When, in October 1972, a House Commerce Committee subcommittee requested the SEC's ITT files, the SEC suddenly transferred the case to the Justice Department together with the files, including documents showing significant contacts between ITT and important Administration officials. WSPF investigated the matter to determine whether this transfer was an illegal obstruction of the House subcommittee, whether anyone committed perjury at the various hearings held by the subcommittees into the transfer, and whether the SEC was improperly influenced to omit a fraud charge from its 1972 case. Also examined was ITT's failure to produce documents from its Washington office in response to the SEC's subpoena.

WSPF also investigated the circumstances under which ITT received favorable tax treatment for its merger with the Hartford Fire Insurance Company. The IRS ruled in October 1969 that ITT had to divest its holdings in that company's shares prior to the stockholders' meeting. Later that month, IRS ruled that a contract involving the "transfer" of these shares to an Italian bank (Mediobanca) was a sufficient sale of the shares under the earlier ruling. In fact, it was questionable whether this contract involved a true sale, especially when the circumstances relating to its negotiation became clear. WSPF has focused on whether these tax rulings were the product of improper influence, whether ITT or its representatives were guilty of *criminally* defrauding the Government by misrepresenting the facts relating to the stock transfer, and whether witnesses who testified about the transaction before the SEC had committed perjury. Although the WSPF inquiry in the area of improper influence is completed, the SEC investigation is continuing with a new evidentiary focus as to the transfer of shares.

During its original investigation the Securities and Exchange Commission had also looked into certain events related to the eventual merger of ITT and Hartford. Although no attempt was made to redo all that the SEC had covered in their investigation, WSPF also conducted its own investigations of these matters.

Finally, the ITT task force also examined testimony before the Senate Foreign Relations Subcommittee on Multinational Corporation's hearings into ITT's activities in Chile during 1970 and 1971 to determine, among other considerations, whether a particular witness had committed perjury. Additionally, the ITT task force spent substantial time investigating possible grand jury perjuries committed during its inquiries.

The investigations of the ITT task force resulted in two criminal cases. In the first case, former Attorney General Richard Kleindienst pleaded guilty on May 16, 1974, to a charge of failing to give accurate testimony at his 1972 confirmation hearings, regarding White House influence on the antitrust suit. He was fined $100 and given a suspended 30-day jail term. In the second case, California Lieutenant Governor Ed Reinecke was convicted after trial on July 27, 1974, of one count of perjury in connection with his testimony at the same hearings. He received a suspended 18-month sentence, and the conviction is now on appeal.

"PLUMBERS" INVESTIGATION

Fielding break-in

In the course of investigating the Watergate case in the spring of 1973, Assistant US Attorneys for the District of Columbia learned from former White House counsel John Dean that a special investigative unit in the White House, known as the "Plumbers," had been responsible for a break-in in September 1971 at the Los Angeles offices of Dr Lewis Fielding, conducted to secure the psychiatric records of Fielding's former patient, Daniel Ellsberg. At the time of the break-in, Ellsberg was under indictment for his role in the alleged theft of the classified "Pentagon Papers."

By the time WSPF was established, the investigation showed that "Plumbers" Gordon Liddy and Howard Hunt had planned the burglary, that some of their Cuban-American associates had carried it out, and that White House aides Egil Krogh and David Young had obtained the approval of another White House staff member, John Ehrlichman, for the project. Hunt had been given immunity from further prosecution after his Watergate conviction and Young had been immunized in order to obtain his cooperation in the Fielding investigation. During the summer of 1973, WSPF's "Plumbers" task force continued this investigation.

On September 4, 1973, a Los Angeles County grand jury which had also been investigating the break-in returned an indictment charging Ehrlichman, Krogh, Liddy, and Young with conspiracy and burglary, Krogh with solicitation to commit burglary, and Ehrlichman with perjury in connection with his testimony before the Los Angeles grand jury. After consultation with WSPF and attorneys for the defendants, the District Attorney in Los Angeles agreed not to press the case to trial pending the outcome of WSPF's investigation.

On October 11, 1973, a Federal grand jury in Washington indicted Krogh on two counts of perjury. These charges were dropped on November 30, following Krogh's plea to a charge of having conspired to violate Dr Fielding's civil rights and his agreement to cooperate with WSPF. On January 24, 1974, Krogh was sentenced to serve two to six years in prison, with all but six months of the term suspended.

WSPF's investigation culminated in the March 7, 1974, indictment of Ehrlichman, former White House aide Charles Colson, Liddy, Bernard Barker, Eugenio Martinez, and Felipe DeDiego on charges of conspiring to violate Dr Fielding's civil rights. Ehrlichman also was charged with lying to the FBI and three counts of perjury in connection with the Federal investigation.

Colson, who also had been indicted in connection with the Watergate cover-up, began discussions with the prosecutors in May to dispose of both matters. An agreement was eventually reached whereby he pleaded guilty, on June 3, to a felony charge of obstructing justice, based on his efforts to obtain and disseminate derogatory information about Ellsberg with intent to impede Ellsberg's pending criminal trial. Colson also agreed to cooperate in WSPF's investigations and prosecutions and on June 21, he was sentenced to a one- to three-year prison term. The other charges against him in the Fielding and Watergate cases were dismissed.

During pretrial proceedings in the Fielding case, Ehrlichman maintained that he had not known in advance that Dr Fielding's office would be broken into and that the effort to collect information about Ellsberg had been a legitimate attempt to protect the national security. Arguing that White House files contained evidence which might support his contentions, his attorneys obtained a subpoena for notes and classified White House documents. When

White House resistance to this subpoena threatened to lead to a dismissal of charges against him, his case was severed for a brief period until White House counsel submitted an affidavit that the files contained no material of an exculpatory nature.

Shortly before trial, DeDiego moved for dismissal of the charges against him, claiming that the evidence which would be used against him was based on immunized testimony he had given to a Florida prosecutor. Judge Gerhard Gesell, to whom the case had been assigned, granted the motion. WSPF successfully appealed this decision on the ground that an evidentiary hearing should precede a dismissal. But the prosecutors later dropped the charges because the immunized testimony raised doubts about the probability of a successful trial. The matter was transferred to Department of Justice lawyers who were "untainted" because they had had no access to DeDiego's immunized account.

The Fielding jury trial lasted three weeks and resulted in a guilty verdict on July 12, 1974, against all remaining defendants with the exception of a not guilty verdict on one of the three perjury charges against Ehrlichman. Judge Gesell, in dismissing one charge against Ehrlichman of lying to the FBI, held that the statute he was accused of violating did not extend to the FBI investigative interview under the kinds of circumstances shown at the trial. On July 31, Barker and Martinez, who had spent substantial time in jail following their conviction in the original Watergate case, received suspended sentences and three years' probation. Liddy was sentenced to a one- to three-year prison term and Ehrlichman to a term of 20 months to five years. All defendants have appealed their convictions.

Other break-in investigations
Newspaper reports in early 1973 suggested that the participants in the Watergate break-in might also have

burglarized the Embassy of Chile in Washington, D.C., on the weekend of May 13–15, 1972, and the homes of Chilean diplomats in New York City earlier in 1972. The "Plumbers" task force investigated these allegations, interviewing the Watergate burglars, officials of the embassy, local police officers, members of a Senate committee staff, former officials of the White House and the Central Intelligence Agency, and journalists. The State Department, CIA, and FBI also provided information in connection with this incident. The investigation did not develop evidence which would form a basis for criminal charges.

WSPF also received allegations from various sources that the White House "Plumbers" or other agents had been responsible for numerous unsolved burglaries in the Washington, D.C. area and elsewhere. The victims of these burglaries had been persons or organizations that might be deemed hostile to the Nixon Administration. The task force's investigations were directed at determining whether there was evidence that the "Plumbers" or other known White House agents had been involved in any of these burglaries. No such evidence was found, and no criminal charges were brought.

Wiretap investigations

Press reports in May 1973 alleged that between 1969 and 1971 the FBI, at the direction of the White House, conducted wiretaps directed at a number of Government officials and newsmen in an effort to discover the sources of unauthorized disclosures of information related to the national security. It was also alleged that some of these wiretaps had been conducted in connection with the investigation of the disclosure of the "Pentagon Papers." These reports prompted Judge W. Matthew Byrne, then presiding at the criminal trial of Daniel Ellsberg, to order the Justice Department to determine whether or not such wiretapping had occurred, and to produce in court all wiretap evidence in any way related to the Ellsberg case.

William D. Ruckelshaus, the new Acting Director of the FBI, launched an intensive investigation to determine whether such wiretap evidence existed. On May 10, 1973, Ruckelshaus informed Judge Byrne that his investigation had determined that such a wiretap project had taken place, that an FBI employee recalled that during the course of a wiretap on the home phone of Dr Morton Halperin[2] at least one telephone conversation of Daniel Ellsberg had been recorded, and that the FBI had not been able to locate the records of these wiretaps. The following day, May 11, Judge Byrne declared a mistrial and dismissed all charges against Ellsberg and his co-defendant on the ground of Government misconduct, citing both the Fielding burglary and the failure of the Government to produce the records of the electronic surveillance of Ellsberg. The following day all records of the wiretap project were located among the White House files of John Ehrlichman and were returned to the FBI. On May 14, 1973, Ruckelshaus held a press conference and revealed that the wiretap project had been conducted from May 1969 to February 1971, that a total of 13 Government officials and four journalists had been subject to electronic surveillance, and that in the summer or fall of 1971 all records of the wiretap project had been removed from the FBI and delivered to Ehrlichman at the White House.

---

2. Dr Halperin, a former assistant to Dr Henry Kissinger, later filed a civil damage suit against Kissinger and others alleging that the wiretapping of Halperin's phone had been illegal. A number of facts concerning the wiretap project have been made public as a result of the depositions taken in the *Halperin* v. *Kissinger* litigation. That case is still pending and further depositions may produce additional public information.

WSPF began its investigation into the events surrounding the wiretap project in the late summer of 1973. Press reports, principally in the *New York Times*, had listed the names of 17 individuals alleged to have been the subjects of these wiretaps. Because some of the Government officials alleged to have been the subjects of these wiretaps had worked in purely domestic areas, WSPF first inquired whether or not these wiretaps had been authorized by the Attorney General and, even if authorized, whether that authorization had been given on the basis of good faith, legitimate national security concerns.[3] It had also been alleged that the wiretap on one of the Government officials had continued after he left the Government to work as a policy adviser for a Democratic Senator then seeking the Presidential nomination. This fact, along with certain documents received by WSPF, also led WSPF to question whether these wiretaps had been used to develop partisan political intelligence, and in addition, whether or not any wiretap information had been "leaked" to the press or otherwise disclosed. (Disclosure of wiretap information is itself a violation of the wiretapping statute.) The continuing investigation finally focused on whether various Government officials had concealed the existence of these wiretaps to obstruct justice—i.e., to prevent the disclosure of the electronic surveillance of Ellsberg—or had concealed the existence of these wiretaps by illegal means such as perjury.

During September and October 1973, WSPF considered requesting direct access to the wiretap files that Ruckelshaus had brought back to the FBI. Special Prosecutor Cox was asked by the FBI to route any such

---

3. Warrantless wiretapping on grounds of domestic (as opposed to foreign) threats to national security was not ruled illegal until a Supreme Court decision in June 1972.

request directly to the Attorney General since the FBI felt that it could not comply with such a request unless instructed to do so by the Attorney General. Cox decided to hold off further negotiations on this issue until after conclusion of the litigation over grand jury access to Presidential tape recordings. In the interim WSPF made an initial determination as to which wiretaps appeared to lack proper national security justification, and attorneys interviewed individuals who had allegedly been the subjects of these questionable wiretaps.

After Cox was fired, Jaworski sought and gained access to the wiretap files. The files were reviewed in December 1973 and the following month, WSPF began presenting witnesses on this matter to the newly empaneled grand jury. The prosecutors examined voluminous FBI records, interviewed current and former FBI and Justice Department personnel, secured grand jury testimony, and spoke with others who were believed to have relevant knowledge.

In the summer of 1974, the prosecutors expanded their investigation by obtaining the assistance of FBI agents assigned to the General Investigative Division.[4] Thereafter, FBI agents conducted most of the initial interviews of witnesses. The investigation of wiretaps initiated by the White House, and the subsequent concealment of the nature and records of that activity, involved the full time of one attorney and part of the time of another over an 18-month period.

---

4. This arrangement was satisfactory to both the FBI and WSPF since the General Investigative Division had jurisdiction to investigate the types of criminal activity in question, and in addition, that division of the FBI had had no previous dealings with the wiretap project, which had been handled exclusively by the FBI's Intelligence Division.

The "Plumbers" task force also looked into a number of allegations of non-FBI wiretapping which was alleged to have been illegal. The most significant of these inquiries was the alleged wiretapping for two weeks of the home telephone of Joseph Kraft, a syndicated columnist, first revealed in June 1973 by John Dean's testimony before the Senate Select Committee. The investigation included interviews of former White House, FBI, and telephone company officials, an interview of Mr Kraft, and a review of relevant White House and FBI documents.

The Counsel to the Special Prosecutor examined the various legal issues involved in these wiretap investigations, and concluded:

> . . . Congress has specifically provided in 18 USC Section 2511 (3) that the statutory prohibition against wiretapping does not apply to measures the President believes necessary "to protect national security information against foreign intelligence activities." Whether any of the taps in question fit within this exception could be debated as a matter of statutory interpretation as well as a matter of actual intention, and there would also be room to contend that the duration of some of the taps showed that even an initially legitimate purpose was altered to an impermissible domestic political goal.
>
> Nevertheless, because of the numerous uncertainties in this area, I would be hesitant to recommend a criminal prosecution of any of the principals involved in initiating what appeared to be "national security" wiretaps.

WSPF investigators and Counsel concluded that at least two of the wiretaps, unlike those addressed in counsel's opinion above, had little, if any, "national security" justification. As to these, however, after investigation by WSPF and the FBI, there was insufficient evidence to bring criminal charges, particularly when weighed against other matters under inquiry by WSPF as to some of the subjects of the wiretap investigation.

Alleged misuse of Federal agencies

Internal Revenue Service (IRS)
In the summer of 1973, the Senate Select Committee heard testimony that members of the White House staff had made various attempts to use the powers of the Internal Revenue Service to further President Nixon's political interests. Former White House counsel John Dean, among others, testified about an "enemies project," which sought "to use the available Federal machinery," including the audit and investigative powers of the IRS, against individuals and organizations viewed as "enemies" and on behalf of individuals viewed as "friends" of the Nixon Administration.

Because these allegations related to abuses of governmental power similar to the activities of the White House "Plumbers," their investigation was assigned in August 1973 to attorneys in the "Plumbers" task force of WSPF. The prosecutors began to examine the matters raised by the Senate hearings and by related allegations. For example, a lawsuit brought by the Center for Corporate Responsibility claimed that its tax-exempt status had been revoked illegally because of its position on various social and economic issues; and various people who had assumed public positions in opposition to Nixon Administration policies complained that they had been subjected to repeated audits or other forms of harassment by the IRS.

The prosecutors began their investigation by familiarizing themselves with IRS operations, including the normal procedures for initiating audits, and by attempting to determine which of the many allegations appeared to have the most substance and, if true, would form the basis for criminal prosecutions. In this process they interviewed a number of former and current IRS officials who provided information on IRS procedures and in some cases also provided facts giving rise to new inquiries.

Although a large number of allegations about possible misuses of the IRS were investigated, the prosecutors made their most extensive inquiries in two areas—the alleged efforts of White House aides in 1972 to get the IRS to audit and harass Lawrence F. O'Brien, Sr, then the chairman for the Democratic National Committee, and alleged attempts by White House officials to influence the IRS to audit various "enemies" of the Administration and act favorably toward certain "friends" of the Administration. During these investigations, the prosecutors received relevant information from the IRS itself, which had conducted its own "in-house" inquiries, and from the staff of the Congressional Joint Committee on Internal Revenue Taxation, which had conducted investigations of matters raised in the Senate hearings.

From the beginning of both of these investigations the prosecutors faced two substantial problems which made any eventual prosecution unlikely. First, even if evidence tending to confirm the allegations was developed (and in many cases it was), it would have been difficult to prove the specific intent required to establish a violation of Federal law, in this case, a conspiracy to defraud the United States in violation of Title 18 USC § 371. In theory, any concerted effort to use Government resources for illegitimate and political—perhaps punitive—purposes would seem to constitute a violation of this provision; but in practice, proof beyond a reasonable doubt of the requisite corrupt intent is difficult where there are objective indicators in each case to support the argument that an audit of an "enemy" was, in fact, in order and consistent with normal IRS standards. Moreover, none of the incidents in question involved evidence of payoffs or other corrupt practices.

A second problem hindering successful investigation arose from the fact that there were numerous inquiries and investigations by other agencies concerning the matters under investigation by WSPF. This often resulted in those principally involved learning substantially all details of the matters WSPF was investigating even before WSPF— and/or the grand juries—came to deal with them. These individuals were able to smooth conflicting testimony and otherwise embroider explanations which made continued investigation by WSPF difficult. Some witnesses who were dealing with WSPF often were close and long-time associates of those under investigation.

Despite these problems the grand jury's investigation did go far in detailing the facts of what had transpired in the area of White House abuse of the IRS. Indeed, in fully investigating the facts of the two specific incidents noted above, WSPF and the grand juries received the testimony of perhaps a hundred or so witnesses. It was concluded ultimately, however, that there was insufficient evidence and/or substantial legal problems mitigating against the bringing of any criminal charges.

White House "Responsiveness Program" and related matters
Evidence obtained by the Senate Select Committee and provided to WSPF in 1974 indicated that as part of a "Responsiveness Program" conducted by a staff unit in the White House, certain White House staff members had attempted in 1972 to channel Federal grants, contracts, loans, subsidies, and other benefits to persons and organizations supporting President Nixon's re-election campaign, and to withhold such benefits from those opposing his candidacy. Two instances of possible criminal conduct were alleged to have taken place pursuant to the "Responsiveness Program": the dropping of an anti-discrimination suit brought by the Equal Employment Opportunity

Commission and the rescinding of a Labor Department subpoena directed at a union which was supporting the President. The prosecutors began their inquiry by obtaining background information and the names of about 30 people who had served as White House contacts in the various agencies for the "Responsiveness Program." The prosecutors then requested the FBI to interview White House staff members allegedly involved, the agency contacts and other witnesses. One of the prosecutors also reviewed the Labor Department's files regarding the rescinded subpoena.

When additional White House documents became available to WSPF in spring of 1975, various files were searched for documents relating to the "Responsiveness Program" in a further effort to learn whether violations of laws had occurred. On the basis of this investigation, it was concluded that certain memoranda obtained by the Senate Select Committee had exaggerated the effect of the "Responsiveness Program" and, accordingly, no criminal charges resulted from WSPF's inquiries.

A similar investigation probed an allegation that the Department of Labor had delayed, and in some matters, also denied the promulgation of various occupational health and safety standards in return for contributions to the President's campaign. A memorandum uncovered by Senate Select Committee investigators appeared to substantiate this charge and led the prosecutors to ask the FBI to interview about 10 individuals about the matter. One witness was also called before the grand jury. It was concluded on the basis of this investigation that no violations of criminal law occurred.

The prosecutors also received allegations in March 1974 that White House officials, for the purpose of assisting President Nixon's re-election efforts, had set up the Federation of Experienced Americans (FEA), an organization sponsoring the elderly citizens, and had made efforts to shift Federal funding to FEA from the National Council on Senior Citizens and the National Council on Aging, two established organizations of the same type, which had not supported the President's policies and were not expected to support his re-election campaign. The General Accounting Office (GAO) had conducted an earlier investigation of FEA and found that White House officials had brought pressure on Federal agencies to award funds to FEA and had helped it to obtain a donation from a corporation. The GAO investigation resulted in the termination of Federal funds to FEA because of financial improprieties. The prosecutors reviewed the GAO's files and, at WSPF's request, FBI agents interviewed more than 40 Government agency employees and White House and FEA officials about possible White House efforts to channel funds to FEA and possible FEA activities in support of the President's 1972 campaign. No evidence was developed to support criminal charges.

Investigation of alleged mistreatment of demonstrators

Investigation into an assault on antiwar demonstrators
Newspaper articles appearing in June 1973, and information obtained in the early stages of the Watergate investigation, suggested that officials of the White House and the Committee to Re-Elect the President had directed an organized assault on antiwar demonstrators on the steps of the Capitol building on the evening of May 3, 1972.

The antiwar demonstration in question featured a number of leading antiwar activists. Coincidentally, but unrelated to the demonstration or the assault, a public viewing of former FBI Director J. Edgar Hoover's coffin in the Capitol Rotunda took place a short distance from the site of the antiwar demonstration.

The early stages of WSPF's investigation, which began in July 1973, revealed that a group of 10 individuals, some of whom had been involved in the break-in of Dr Fielding's office in California, and some of whom subsequently became involved in the illegal entries into the Democratic National Committee headquarters at the Watergate complex, had been present during the assault. Their transportation from Miami was financed with $3,200 in campaign funds.

On the basis of this and other evidence, WSPF conducted an extensive investigation into this incident because of the allegations that the assault had been ordered by White House officials and because of the close connection between this event and the first Watergate break-in three weeks later. It was also considered significant that the original $1 million plan from which the Watergate burglary evolved included a proposal for mugging squads to rough up demonstrators. Thus, the investigation sought to determine any existence or implementation of a general plan to use paid operatives for the purpose of violent activity against demonstrators and other anti-Administration activists.

Accordingly, more than 150 witnesses were interviewed including victims of the assault, witnesses to it, police officers, and White House and CRP personnel. Witnesses who resided a long distance from Washington and those of less significance were interviewed by the FBI. Of those interviewed, some testified before the grand jury. A request for a thorough search of White House documents relevant to this investigation was made by Cox in October 1973, but relevant materials were not made available to WSPF until the spring of 1975. This investigation consumed a substantial portion of the time of two attorneys over a six-month period. No criminal charges were brought.

Investigation of alleged mistreatment of demonstrators at
Presidential appearances
A newspaper story in August 1973 alleged that persons
who appeared to be demonstrators against or opponents of
the Nixon Administration had been excluded or removed
from the public coliseum in Charlotte, N.C., on the occasion of the President's appearance there on October 15,
1971, and that this activity had been conducted by local
volunteers from the Veterans of Foreign Wars recruited by
White House advancemen. The prosecutors had previously
been told that advancemen had made similar attempts to
keep demonstrators away from the President as he made
public appearances around the country, and they then
interviewed a former advanceman about these general
allegations. After the publication of the newspaper story,
WSPF received from a citizens' group a report containing
specific allegations of mistreatment of demonstrators at
various Presidential appearances, including the Charlotte
incident, from 1971 to 1973.

WSPF investigated these charges through office and
FBI interviews of former CRP and White House officials
including the advancemen, and through an examination of
White House tapes and documents which became available
in the spring of 1975. Some of the witnesses were questioned before a grand jury.

In mid-September 1973, Cox learned that the Civil
Rights Division of the Justice Department was also investigating some of these same allegations. As a result,
arrangements were made between this office and the Civil
Rights Division for a joint effort in which investigative
responsibilities were divided between the two offices. Major
witnesses, however, were interviewed by two attorneys working together, one from WSPF and one from Civil Rights. The
investigation, conducted over approximately a three-month
period, did not result in the proof of criminal activity.

Investigation of President Nixon's tax returns

Newspaper articles appearing in the summer and fall of 1973 indicated that President Nixon had paid minimal Federal taxes on substantial income earned during the period of 1969 to 1972 because of a deduction he had taken for the purported gift of his Pre-Presidential papers to the National Archives. The White House claimed that the papers had been given before the effective date of a 1969 tax reform law that greatly reduced the amount allowed as a tax deduction for such gifts. After considerable public interest and speculation, President Nixon made public in December his tax returns for the four previous years, along with supporting financial data and a request that the Congressional Joint Committee on Internal Revenue Taxation determine whether he owed additional taxes. Both the Joint Committee and the Internal Revenue Service investigated the matter.

Late in March 1974, IRS notified the Special Prosecutor that its inquiry had reached an impasse because of conflicts in the statements of those principally involved in the matter, and suggested that WSPF conduct a grand jury investigation. While the IRS inquiry indicated possible violations of law by former White House staff members whose activities were clearly within the terms of WSPF's jurisdiction, it also indicated the possible involvement of others who were not covered by the language in WSPF's charter. To avoid any possible ambiguity, Jaworski requested and received from Attorney General Saxbe specific authorization to conduct the entire investigation. For about seven months WSPF conducted an investigation to determine the facts concerning the alleged gift and whether efforts had been made to conceal the circumstances of the transaction. To this end, the prosecutors interviewed and called before the grand jury a number of witnesses, including former White House staff members and officials of the General

Services Administration and its National Archives and Records Service. They also received assistance from others who had looked into some of the questions, including the IRS, the Joint Committee, and the House Judiciary Committee.

The WSPF investigation resulted in the filing of charges against three people. Former White House deputy counsel Edward L. Morgan pleaded guilty on November 8, 1974, to conspiring to defraud the United States by participating in the preparation of backdated documents. He was sentenced to two years imprisonment, all but four months of which was suspended. On February 19, 1975, the grand jury filed a four-count indictment charging Frank DeMarco, a Los Angeles lawyer who had helped prepare President Nixon's tax returns, and Ralph G. Newman, a Chicago book dealer and appraiser who had estimated the value of his papers for tax purposes, with having engaged along with Morgan in a conspiracy to defraud the United States. The indictment also charged DeMarco with making false statements to IRS agents and with obstructing the Joint Committee's inquiry, and Newman with assisting in the preparation of a false document filed with a tax return. After extensive legal argument, including an unsuccessful mandamus petition by WSPF to the Court of Appeals, the defendants obtained separate trial settings, DeMarco in Los Angeles and Newman in Chicago. As of the writing of this Report, the Los Angeles trial was scheduled for September 16 and the Chicago trial for October 28, 1975.

CAMPAIGN CONTRIBUTIONS

Investigation of 1972 campaign financing and related matters

Beginning in June 1973, the campaign contributions task force systematically examined the campaign finances of major 1972 Republican and Democratic Presidential candidates. This examination included the investigation of several hundred separate transactions, including corporate and labor union contributions, recipients' non-reporting of contributions and expenditures, and alleged *quid pro quo* relationships between contributions and Government actions.

The task force began its inquiries on the basis of the following major sources of information:

(1) A list of persons who made large contributions to President Nixon's re-election campaign before April 7, 1972—the effective date of a new campaign law which required that contributions be reported publicly. The existence of this list, which was kept by the President's secretary, was initially disclosed in a civil suit brought by Common Cause against the Finance Committee to Re-Elect the President (FCRP). WSPF later obtained the list from the White House.

(2) Reports of pre-April 7 contributions to several Democratic candidates, which the candidates had made public.

(3) Reports of post-April 7 contributions to candidates of both parties which had been filed with the General Accounting Office pursuant to the new law.

(4) Referrals from the Internal Revenue Service.

(5) Information obtained in the Watergate investigation about the sources and disposition of campaign funds used in the Watergate break-in and cover-up.

(6) Newspaper articles, letters from citizens (many of them anonymous), and similar sources.

A variety of investigative methods were used. The prosecutors interviewed major Republican and Democratic fundraisers, including Herbert Kalmbach of FCRP, who cooperated with the office under an agreement involving his guilty plea to two charges (described elsewhere in this section). Agents of the FBI and IRS examined the campaign financial records of the major Presidential candidates and those Congressional candidates whose campaign finances, for various reasons, became relevant to matters directly within the jurisdiction of the Special Prosecutor. The prosecutors sent letters to about 50 known contributors asking them to telephone the office and answer certain questions. Many contributors were interviewed in person in WSPF's offices. FBI agents interviewed hundreds of employees and financial officers of corporations and unions and examined bank and corporate records; IRS agents took similar steps in cases that seemed to involve possible tax violations. In some cases, particularly when there was a suspicion of an explicit *quid quo pro* relationship between contributions and Government actions, WSPF attorneys conducted interviews of contributors, fundraisers, and Government officials. Witnesses were also called before the grand jury, especially when it appeared that attempts were being made to obstruct an investigation.

An important source of information in these inquiries was the disclosure by a number of corporations of their own illegal contributions. On July 6, 1973, American Airlines' board chairman told WSPF and publicly announced that the corporation had made an illegal contribution of corporate funds to the President's re-election campaign. Special Prosecutor Cox then issued a public invitation to other corporate executives to make similar disclosures, promising that:

> [W]hen corporate officers come forward voluntarily and early to disclose illegal political contributions to candidates of either party, their voluntary acknowledgement will be

considered as a mitigating circumstance in deciding what charges to bring.

Several corporations responded to this invitation shortly after it was issued, and others made similar disclosures in the ensuing months (in some cases after learning that they were under investigation). The corporations were required to disclose all corporate contributions to candidates for Federal office within the period of the then statute of limitations (1968–1973). The corporations were also required to disclose the basic method they had used to generate the contributed funds, including accumulations of cash in political "slush funds," usually from overseas sources, and the use of bonus payments and expense accounts to reimburse employees for contributions made in their own names. Interviews were conducted to determine those corporate officers who were aware of, or authorized, the contribution and also to learn what matters the corporation had pending before Federal Government agencies. The prosecutors also investigated the possibility of pressure on employees to donate to corporate "good Government funds" which could be used to make otherwise legal political contributions. In addition to the criminal charges WSPF brought against such corporate "volunteers," other agencies such as IRS and the Securities and Exchange Commission conducted investigations and took action as a result of these disclosures to WSPF.

On October 17, 1973, Cox announced an office policy on bringing charges against corporate officers who had made voluntary disclosure of corporate contributions: the corporation would be charged with violating Section 610 of Title 18 of the US Code, which prohibits corporate contributions, and the primarily responsible corporate officer would be charged under the same statute with consenting to the making of such a contribution. The officer's cooperation in bringing the violation to WSPF's attention would be reflected in a one-count misdemeanor charge of "non-willful" consent, as distinct from the felony of "willful" consent, and in a decision not to charge other officers or include additional counts. Variations of this pattern would be based on unusual degrees of cooperation, on obstructive conduct, or on other unique circumstances. The corporations which made voluntary full disclosure of illegal contributions at a point when little or no investigative work had been done regarding their activities were charged and sentenced as follows:

- On October 17, 1973, American Airlines pleaded guilty to a one-count violation of Section 610 and received a fine of $5,000. The board chairman was not charged because he had been the first corporate officer to make such a disclosure, and had done so before Cox had issued his invitation.
- On the same date, Goodyear Tire and Rubber Company pleaded guilty to one count of violating Section 610 and was fined $5,000; the chairman of Goodyear, Russell DeYoung, pleaded guilty to a one-count misdemeanor, Section 610 violation, and was fined $1,000.
- On the same date, Minnesota Mining and Manufacturing Company pleaded guilty to a one-count Section 610 violation and was fined $3,000; the company's chairman, Harry Heltzer, pleaded guilty to a one-count misdemeanor of violating Section 610 and was fined $500.
- On November 12, 1973, Braniff Airways Inc., pleaded guilty to one count of violating Section 610 and was fined $5,000; Braniff's chairman, Harding L. Lawrence, pleaded guilty to a one-count misdemeanor, Section 610 charge, and was fined $1,000.
- On November 13, 1973, Ashland Petroleum Gabon Corp., a subsidiary of Ashland Oil, Inc., pleaded guilty to

a one-count Section 610 violation and was fined $5,000. Because his disclosure had closely followed American Airlines, Ashland's chairman, Orin E. Atkins, was allowed to plead *nolo contendere* to a one-count Section 610 misdemeanor charge and was fined $1,000.

- On the same date, Gulf Oil Corporation pleaded guilty to one count of violating Section 610 and received a $5,000 fine; Claude C. Wild, Jr, a vice-president of Gulf, pleaded guilty to a one-count misdemeanor under Section 610 and was fined $1,000.

- On December 4, 1973, Phillips Petroleum Company pleaded guilty to one count of violating Section 610 and was fined $5,000; chairman William W. Keeler pleaded guilty to a one-count misdemeanor, Section 610 violation and received a $1,000 fine.

- On December 19, 1973, Carnation Company pleaded guilty to a one-count Section 610 violation and was fined $5,000; its chairman, H. Everett Olson, pleaded guilty to a one-count misdemeanor violation of Section 610 and received a $1,000 fine.

- On March 7, 1974, Diamond International Corporation pleaded guilty to a one-count violation of Section 610 and received a $5,000 fine; Ray Dubrowin, the corporation's vice-president, pleaded guilty to a one-count misdemeanor under Section 610 and was fined $1,000.

- On June 27, 1974, National By-Products, Inc., pleaded guilty to one count of violating Section 610 and was fined $1,000. The responsible officer was not charged because the contribution had been very small, his disclosure had been motivated entirely by conscience, and under the circumstances of the contribution, success in an investigation here had been highly unlikely.

- On October 8, 1974, Greyhound Corporation pleaded guilty to a one-count, Section 610 violation and was fined $5,000. No corporate officer was charged because there was substantial evidence that those involved had believed their conduct to be legal and had relied on the advice of counsel to that effect.

- On December 30, 1974, Charles N. Huseman, of HMS Electric Corporation, pleaded guilty to a one-count violation of Section 610 as a misdemeanor and was fined $1,000. The corporation was not charged because it had been acquired by another corporation and dissolved after the violation.

- On January 28, 1975, Ratrie, Robbins, and Schweitzer, Inc., pleaded guilty to a one-count, Section 610 violation and was fined $2,500. Harry Ratrie and Augustus Robbins, III, each pleaded guilty to a one-count, Section 610 misdemeanor and received a suspended sentence. Two officers were charged because they appeared to be equally culpable.

As the work of the task force progressed, it became clear that there were different degrees of voluntary cooperation. The early volunteers were aware that they might face investigation because their names or the names of their corporations appeared on campaign records WSPF had obtained. Rather than constructing "cover stories," they decided to acknowledge their conduct. Some other "volunteers" did not have to guess that their contributions might be under investigation. WSPF had already begun active inquiries when they decided to make their disclosures. These belated "volunteers" were charged and sentenced as follows:

- On May 1, 1974, Northrop Corporation pleaded guilty to a one-count violation of Section 611 of Title 18, which prohibits campaign contributions by Government contractors, and was fined $5,000. Northrop was charged under this statute because a large percentage of its total business was under Government contract. Northrop's chairman, Thomas V. Jones, pleaded guilty to a charge of willfully aiding and abetting in the illegal contribution and was fined $5,000. James Allen pleaded guilty to a one-count misdemeanor under Section 610 and received a $1,000 fine. Two officers were charged, one of them with a felony, because of obstructive conduct in the course of the investigation.

- On May 6, 1974, Lehigh Valley Cooperative Farmers pleaded guilty to one count of violating Section 610 and was fined $5,000. The Cooperative's president, Richard L. Allison, pleaded guilty on May 17, to a one-count, Section 610 misdemeanor and received a $1,000 fine which was suspended, and Francis X. Carroll pleaded guilty May 28 to a misdemeanor charge of aiding and abetting a violation of Section 610, receiving a suspended sentence. Two persons were charged in this matter because of relatively minor obstructive conduct.

- On September 17, 1974, LBC&W, Inc. pleaded guilty to a one-count violation of Section 611 and received a $5,000 fine; a substantial portion of the firm's total business was under Government contract. William Lyles, Sr, pleaded guilty to two misdemeanor counts of violating Section 610 and was fined $2,000.

- On October 23, 1974, Time Oil Corporation pleaded guilty to two counts of violating Section 610 and was fined $5,000; its president, Raymond Abendroth, pleaded guilty to two misdemeanor Section 610 counts and was fined $2,000.

- On December 20, 1974, Ashland Oil, Inc. pleaded guilty to five counts of violating Section 610 and was fined $25,000. This second prosecution of Ashland resulted from its failure to make full disclosure during the initial investigation. No corporate officer was charged because the officers were not the persons primarily responsible for withholding the information.

Some alleged corporate donors were prosecuted solely as a result of investigations with no voluntary disclosure. A referral from the IRS resulted on October 19, 1973, in the charging of Dwayne Andreas and the First Interoceanic Corporation with four counts of violating Section 610. They were acquitted by a judge in Federal court in Minnesota on July 12, 1974.

An investigation into the contribution activity of American Ship Building Company resulted in the indictment on April 5, 1974, of the corporation and its chairman, George M. Steinbrenner, III, on a charge of conspiring to make corporate contributions to several candidates and campaign organizations. In addition, the corporation was charged with one count of violating Section 610, and Steinbrenner was charged with five felony counts of violating Section 610, two counts of aiding and abetting the making of false statements to criminal investigators, four counts of obstructing justice and two counts of obstructing a criminal investigation. John H. Melcher, Jr, another officer of the corporation, pleaded guilty April 18, 1974, to a charge of being an accessory after the fact to a corporate contribution and was fined $2,500. After plea negotiations with WSPF, American Ship Building pleaded guilty on August 23 to the charges against it and was fined $20,000. On the same date, Steinbrenner pleaded guilty to the felony conspiracy charge and to a charge of being an accessory after the fact to a corporate contribution, receiving a fine of $15,000. The remaining charges against Steinbrenner were dropped following his plea of guilty.

The investigation into the sources of campaign funds which came to be used in the Watergate cover-up resulted in a guilty plea of Tim M. Babcock, an executive of Occidental Petroleum Corp. and former Governor of Montana, on a charge of making a campaign contribution in another person's name, on December 10, 1974. He was sentenced to a year in prison, with all but four months suspended, and a $1,000 fine. His sentence is now on appeal on the question of whether the particular sentencing provision applied here legally permits imprisonment.

The investigation into corporate and union contributions and other illegal activities by donors of campaign funds resulted in no additional prosecutions as of September 1975 (although a few matters are still open). A few other corporations were found to have made relatively small contributions of corporate funds and were not prosecuted because of the small amounts involved. The prosecutors reviewed all contributions identified with unions or their officers in search of patterns that might indicate a union source for individual contributions, but found only one suspicious pattern; the investigation did not develop sufficient evidence to bring charges.

The task force also looked into possible illegal conduct of people and organizations receiving campaign funds on behalf of candidates. The investigation of American Ship Building Company's contributions resulted in a plea of guilty by "DKI for '74," a committee supporting the re-election of Senator Daniel Inouye, to a charge of failing to report a contribution. The sentence was suspended. The investigation and eventual disclosure of a contribution of Time Oil Corporation resulted in a plea of guilty on June 11, 1975, by former Representative Wendell Wyatt, who had headed the Oregon Committee to Re-Elect the President, to a charge of failing to report a campaign expenditure. He was fined $750.

The investigation of the activities of the Finance Committee to Re-Elect the President resulted in a plea of guilty by its former chairman, Maurice Stans, who had served as Secretary of Commerce in the Nixon Administration, to three counts of failure to report contributions and expenditures of the Committee and two

counts of accepting corporate contributions, all misde-
meanors. Stans was fined $5,000. No criminal charges were
brought against other FCRP officials or fundraisers for
other 1972 candidates.

The task force also investigated over 30 allegations of
improper influence on Government actions by contributors to the President's 1972 campaign, including Justice
Department actions in antitrust matters, Environmental
Protection Agency decisions in enforcement proceedings,
Price Commission and Cost of Living Council rulings, the
awarding of bank charters, decisions on airline routes and
mergers, decisions on product safety standards, the exercise
of the President's clemency power, the handling of a criminal
prosecution, decisions on oil import allocations, and a
decision to raise milk price supports (discussed elsewhere in
this section). None of these inquiries developed sufficient
evidence to support criminal charges.

Other allegations involving Democratic campaign
financing were investigated, including a charge that the
Democratic National Committee had received corporate
contributions in the form of discounts in the settlement of
its 1968 campaign debt. These inquiries did not produce
sufficient evidence to support criminal charges. An investigation into the failure of the Democratic National
Committee to report correctly a large contribution
resulted in no charges because the statute of limitations, as
amended retroactively in 1974, barred prosecution.

Investigation into alleged sales of ambassadorships
Information obtained from major campaign contributors
and fundraisers in early summer 1973, and a document
obtained from the White House, suggested that officials of
the White House and the Finance Committee to Re-Elect
the President (FCRP) might have promised ambassadorial
appointments in return for large campaign contributions. A

full-scale inquiry into the alleged sales of ambassadorships commenced in the autumn of 1973.

The investigation centered on possible promises to certain individuals who had made large contributions to President Nixon's re-election. Because the prosecutors felt that favor-selling public officials would be more culpable by reason of their public trust than favor-seeking contributors, if such illegal conduct had occurred, the investigation initially focused on obtaining the testimony of the contributors. However, the first admission that an ambassadorship had been promised in return for a campaign contribution came from fundraiser Herbert Kalmbach, who pleaded guilty on February 24, 1974, to a charge of promising employment as a reward for political activity. Kalmbach, who pleaded guilty to another charge (described elsewhere in this section) at the same time, was sentenced to six-months imprisonment.

On March 14, 1974, the grand jury subpoenaed White House documents relating to the possible appointments and contributions of four persons, and the White House supplied a number of documents which provided additional evidence. Some of the contributors eventually cooperated with the office and furnished information, as did former FCRP chairman Maurice Stans in connection with his guilty plea to other charges (described elsewhere in this section). The contributors, former White House officials, and campaign fundraisers were questioned before the grand jury. Although contributors of large campaign sums obviously received Administration responses to their desires to serve as ambassadors, a crime is not proved unless the prosecution can show a prior *quid pro quo* arrangement, i.e., a prior commitment of support for the position in exchange for a forthcoming contribution. Such proof is available only if one of the participants in such a conversation admits the express commitment. However, each official and fundraiser involved denied having made promises of appointments and WSPF was unable to prove the contrary. Although one matter was still under investigation as this Report was written, the evidence in other matters was insufficient to support any additional criminal charges.

"Townhouse" investigation

Between 1970 and 1972, press accounts indicated that the White House had sponsored a secret program for raising and disbursing funds for selected Republican candidates in the 1970 Congressional elections. This program operated from a Washington townhouse and ultimately became known as "Townhouse." The operation was not thought to be a matter within WSPF's jurisdiction until August 1973, when a separate investigation brought to light more details about the manner in which it had been conducted. During the early fall of 1973, Attorney General Richardson informally referred the "Townhouse" investigation to WSPF, and the referral was formalized by Acting Attorney General Bork in January 1974.

The "Townhouse" inquiry began with interviews of Jack Gleason, a former White House aide who had played a principal role in the project. He supplied records showing that over $3,000,000 had been received and disbursed during the operation. Subsequent investigation revealed these details: fundraiser Herbert Kalmbach had obtained pledges of large amounts from various contributors, informing them that Gleason would contact them about payment; Gleason then instructed the contributors to send their checks to him, and he forwarded the funds to particular campaigns as instructed by members of the White House staff; he reported principally to White House aide Harry Dent who, in turn, reported to other officials at the White House.

After research into the legality of the operation, the prosecutors concluded that those involved had constituted a political committee which had unlawfully failed to elect officers and file financial reports. Their failure to do so, the secrecy with which they conducted their operations, and the large amounts of money involved led the prosecutors to initiate a grand jury investigation in the fall of 1973. In connection with the grand jury's inquiry, the prosecutors asked the White House to supply additional "Townhouse" records which had been transferred to White House files. The records were not produced until March 1974.

Kalmbach, who was cooperating with WSPF in a number of its investigations, pleaded guilty on February 25, 1974, to a felony violation of the Corrupt Practices Act. Thereafter, he furnished additional documents from his files regarding the "Townhouse" project and provided further information during office interviews and grand jury appearances.

On November 15 and December 11, 1974, respectively, Gleason and Dent pleaded guilty to misdemeanor violations of the Corrupt Practices Act. Both received sentences of one month's probation. The prosecutors also looked into the possible liability of others involved in the 1970 "Townhouse" project, but brought no further charges.

Milk fund investigation

In late July 1973, WSPF's campaign contributions task force began investigating possible illegal activities involving Associated Milk Producers, Inc. (AMPI), the Nation's largest organization of dairy farmers. The office's interest in the matter resulted from press reports and the filing of a civil suit by Ralph Nader alleging that a 1971 Administration decision to raise milk price supports had been influenced by an AMPI commitment of substantial funds to President Nixon's 1972 campaign.

The attorneys assigned to this investigation functioned for most purposes as a separate task force within the office. They began by interviewing AMPI's general manager and other employees, and examining evidence obtained in the Nader suit. Then, having learned from a former AMPI employee of a series of diversions of AMPI funds which evidently had been contributed illegally to various political candidates, they obtained grand jury testimony by AMPI officials Bob Lilly and Robert Isham who, under immunity, provided information concerning four areas of possible criminal conduct by persons associated with AMPI.

The first of these areas was the allegation that AMPI had concealed a 1969 contribution of $100,000 to President Nixon's 1972 campaign by using a "dummy" to deliver the funds. Investigation of the 1969 payment resulted in charges against AMPI and Harold Nelson, its former general manager. Nelson's plea of guilty, described more fully below, included admissions that he had made the payment in order to gain "access" to the White House for AMPI and that he had attempted to conceal the ultimate source of the contribution.

On the basis of information they had received, the prosecutors also investigated other political contributions by AMPI. The investigation uncovered evidence of numerous contributions, usually made through conduits to hide the true source of the money. For example, it appeared that AMPI employees, attorneys, or consultants had made contributions in their own names and then, by prior agreement, had been reimbursed by AMPI in the form of "bonuses" or fees. AMPI also disguised political contributions by using corporate funds to pay for services provided to candidates by third parties, and assigning its employees to work in favored campaigns while continuing to be paid by AMPI. The evidence gathered in this part of the investigation led to a number of criminal dispositions:

- On July 24, 1974, David Parr, formerly special counsel to AMPI, pleaded guilty to a felony conspiracy to make corporate contributions. In acknowledging his guilt, he admitted his role in causing AMPI to contribute a total of $220,000 to eight different candidates in 1968, 1970, and 1972. Parr was fined $10,000 and sentenced to two years imprisonment. All but four months of the prison term were suspended.

- AMPI's former general manager Nelson pleaded guilty on July 31, 1974, to felony charges of conspiracy to make corporate contributions and making an illegal payment to a public official. He admitted that he had caused AMPI to make contributions totalling $330,000 to seven different campaign funds in 1968, 1970, and 1972, and had approved a payment to another party in 1971, allegedly for the benefit of John Connally, Secretary of the Treasury. Nelson was sentenced to pay a $10,000 fine and serve a two-year prison term, with all but four months suspended.

- On August 1, 1974, AMPI pleaded guilty to conspiracy to make corporate campaign contributions, and the making of five such contributions totalling $280,000, and was fined $35,000 maximum.

- Norman Sherman and John Valentine, who had operated a computer service and had received $84,000 from AMPI for services provided to several candidates, each pleaded guilty on August 12, 1974, to misdemeanor charges of aiding and abetting illegal corporate contributions. Each was fined $500.

- Jack Chestnut, the manager of Hubert Humphrey's 1970 Senate campaign in Minnesota, was indicted on December 23, 1974, for feloniously aiding and abetting a corporate contribution by arranging for AMPI to pay for the services of a New York advertising firm to the Humphrey campaign. At WSPF's request after the indictment, Chestnut's trial was conducted in May 1975 by the US Attorney's office for the Southern District of New York, and resulted in his conviction and a four-month prison sentence. The conviction is now on appeal.

- On December 19, 1974, Stuart Russell, an Oklahoma City attorney retained by AMPI, was indicted for conspiracy and two counts of aiding and abetting the making of corporate contributions. The charges were based on evidence of his major role as a conduit for political contributions of AMPI funds. He was convicted in July 1975 on all three felony counts after a trial in San Antonio, Texas and received a two-year prison sentence. His appeal is pending.

The third area of investigation involving AMPI concerned events surrounding the Administration's 1971 decision to raise milk price supports and AMPI's commitment of funds for the 1972 campaign, but despite an extensive probe, the prosecutors were unable to obtain sufficient evidence to recommend criminal charges against anyone.

The final area of the investigation of AMPI's activities concerned the allegation that former Treasury Secretary Connally had accepted illegal payments from AMPI following the Administration's 1971 decision to increase milk price support levels. This investigation resulted in the charge against Nelson, described above, to which he pleaded guilty. In addition, Jake Jacobsen, a Texas attorney formerly retained by AMPI, was charged on February 21, 1974, with having made false declarations before the grand jury. This charge was dismissed as technically defective on May 3, but Jacobsen was indicted again on July 29, 1974, for making an illegal payment to a public official. He pleaded guilty on August 7 and is awaiting sentence. Connally was also named as a defendant with Jacobsen in the July 29 indictment. He was charged with receiving illegal payments on two occasions while he was Secretary of the Treasury, conspiring with Jacobsen to commit perjury and obstruct justice in connection with investigations of those payments, and making false declarations to the grand jury. Prior to trial, the court ruled that the charges of accepting illegal payments should be tried first and separately. Connally was tried on these charges and found not guilty by a jury on April 17, 1975. Because the jury had also heard all the evidence the prosecutors possessed for any future trial on the other charges against Connally, those charges were dismissed on April 18.

Hughes-Rebozo investigation

In October 1973, WSPF began receiving from the Internal Revenue Service the preliminary results of its investigation into an unreported cash contribution of $100,000 by industrialist Howard R. Hughes delivered by a Hughes representative to Charles G. Rebozo, a close friend of President Nixon. The funds had been delivered in two equal installments in 1970, but according to Rebozo's public explanation, the identical cash had been returned to Hughes in June 1973.

Since July 1973, the Senate Select Committee had also been conducting an investigation which was essentially parallel to that of the IRS. In December 1973 and thereafter, the Committee questioned numerous witnesses in Executive Session about the Hughes contribution. In late March one witness, Herbert W. Kalmbach, formerly the personal attorney for Richard Nixon, alleged that on April 30, 1973, Rebozo had told him of having disbursed some of the Hughes money to a friend and family members of the President, and others. Investigators also searched to see whether the Hughes cash that had been returned by Rebozo in June 1973 bore serial numbers that indicated the cash had been in public circulation at the time of the two alleged deliveries by Hughes' representative to Rebozo in 1970.

On the basis of Senate and IRS information, the Special Prosecutor's office launched a wider investigation. Although the charter of the Special Prosecutor's office included authority to investigate all matters arising out of the 1972 Presidential election campaign, for which, according to Rebozo, the Hughes contribution had been intended, it was determined that there should be some clarification of WSPF's jurisdiction to investigate the matter. By letter dated April 15, 1974, the Attorney General specifically assigned to the Special Prosecutor the responsibility for conducting an investigation into the Hughes contribution and related matters. At about the same time, the Internal Revenue Service referred its investigation to the Special Prosecutor along with an interim report recommending a grand jury inquiry to resolve conflicts in the testimony of witnesses about the delivery and purpose of the Hughes money, as well as its possible use, and to seek evidence of other such secret contributions.

Three broad categories of inquiry were pursued: any possible bribery and campaign contribution violations, any income tax violations, and any perjury or false statements arising from prior testimony. A grand jury investigation was begun in late April 1974 with the issuance of numerous subpoenas for documents.

The Senate investigation also continued and in May 1974, a former aide to H. R. Haldeman, Lawrence M. Higby, testified before the Committee that Haldeman had described to him an offer which the President had made to pay $400,000 from funds under Rebozo's control, for Haldeman's anticipated legal fees.

The Select Committee's investigation ended in July 1974, when the Committee published a lengthy staff report describing the information disclosed during its investigation. The report included allegations: (1) that in June 1972 Rebozo had used funds which were left from the 1968 campaign and kept in one of his bank accounts, to pay for diamond earrings for Mrs Nixon; and (2) that Rebozo had paid for a swimming pool and related improvements to the President's Key Biscayne residences with about $25,000 cash from unknown sources in 1972.

During May and June 1974, the Special Prosecutor's office obtained all documents from the files of the Senate Select Committee and the Internal Revenue Service relating to Rebozo's finances. On the basis of these materials, the grand jury inquiry was broadened and nearly 200 subpoenas for documents were issued between April 1974 and July 1975. In addition, 28 witnesses testified before the grand jury, 75 persons were questioned by the Special Prosecutor's office and 47 persons were interviewed in the field by a team of specially detailed agents of the Internal Revenue Service. In all, 123 different persons were questioned, many of them repeatedly. Included among those questioned were officials and employees of the White House, the Finance Committee to Re-Elect the President, Hughes' Summa Corporation, the Key Biscayne Bank, and many others.

The IRS team also assisted the Special Prosecutor's office in evaluating the voluminous financial records obtained. Between April and December 1974, the agents and Assistant Special Prosecutors analyzed thousands of pages of records received from more than 240 sources.

Secondary sources of information also were systematically and exhaustively utilized. This included records from banks, accountants, attorneys, various business partners and associates, business firms, and so forth. Second, voluminous records were reviewed of telephone calls, travel, meetings with Administration officials, and correspondence with various persons. Third, persons suspected of making secret contributions were questioned and their documents reviewed. Fourth, tapes and hundreds of memoranda and other documents from the White House files were studied for any references to relevant financial transactions or any actions involving soliciting or use of funds for President Nixon.

Extensive investigation was undertaken concerning the source and application of all funds which required examination in order to resolve the matters raised in the Senate Select Committee materials. Documents and information were obtained which had not been available to the Committee, and they helped resolve some questions which were raised by the Senate report.

Investigation was also pursued into the suggestion in an April 17, 1973, Presidential tape that Rebozo maintained a secret fund of about $300,000. At the trial of the Watergate cover-up defendants, prosecutors used a transcript of this tape of a conversation among President Nixon and his aides H. R. Haldeman and John D. Ehrlichman. In the conversation, President Nixon offered to pay $200,000 to $300,000 for their legal fees from funds to be provided by Rebozo.

After all investigation was completed, and the evidence had been evaluated by the prosecutors who ran the investigation and by the General Counsel's office of the Internal Revenue Service, it was concluded by the prosecutors that the evidence would not support an indictment.

National Hispanic Finance Committee investigation

Information provided by the Senate Select Committee indicated the possibility that former staff members of the White House, the Committee to Re-Elect the President, and the National Hispanic Finance Committee (an arm of the Finance Committee to Re-Elect the President) had tried to influence the Government's grant-making and contracting processes to obtain the support of members of the Spanish-speaking community for the President's re-election. Although these allegations were similar to those related to the Administration's "Responsiveness Program" (see discussion of "Responsiveness Program" above), they were investigated by personnel of a different task force because they seemed to involve principally representatives of the President's campaign organization.

WSPF investigated several allegations of possible criminal conduct including:

- That the award of Government contracts to a particular firm had been curtailed because the firm's president had declined to support President Nixon's re-election campaign; one means of this curtailment had been the "graduation" of the firm beyond the eligibility requirement for the Small Business Administration (SBA) program which awards Government contracts to minority-owned firms outside the normal bidding process.
- That a builder who was having legal difficulties, in a housing program for low-income families subsidized by the Federal Housing Administration, had been solicited for a $100,000 contribution in return for the clearing up of his legal problems.
- That a prominent Mexican-American citizen had been offered a Federal judgeship in exchange for a campaign contribution.
- That improper influence, possibly involving persons connected with the Hispanic Finance Committee, had existed in the awarding of grants, SBA loans, and Government contracts.

These inquiries consumed about one year of an attorney's time, but did not produce sufficient evidence to support criminal charges.

RELATIONS WITH PRESIDENTS AND WHITE HOUSE STAFFS

EFFORTS TO OBTAIN EVIDENCE

Early requests for documents

During his confirmation hearings in May 1973, Attorney General designate Elliot Richardson expressed his belief that the Special Prosecutor would gain access to Presidential papers without litigation. He said:

> [F]rom all I have seen and from the President's statements, he intends that whatever should be made public in terms of the public interest in these investigations should be disclosed.

Nevertheless, at Cox's insistence, in order to formalize and reinforce his independence to challenge any withholding of information, the guidelines for his office granted the Special Prosecutor "full authority" in "determining whether or not to contest the assertion of 'executive privilege.'"

The first exchange of letters occurred on May 30, when Cox wrote to White House counsel J. Fred Buzhardt to confirm an earlier telephone request that all White House files related to the Special Prosecutor's investigation be kept "secure." Buzhardt responded that certain files had been placed under the protection of the FBI on April 30, but that the "handling, protection and disposition of Presidential Papers is, of course, a matter for the decision of the President." In the months that followed, the White House repeatedly delayed their responses to the Special Prosecutor's requests for documents by citing the need for a personal decision of the President.

On June 6, Cox and Special Consultant James Vorenberg met with Buzhardt, White House counsel Leonard Garment, and Charles Alan Wright, a consultant to the White House counsel's office. At this meeting Wright stated his understanding that the doctrine of executive privilege gave the President an absolute right to refuse to disclose in either judicial or congressional proceedings any confidential communications between the President and his advisers and any memoranda generated by White House staff members concerning the constitutional duties of the President.

The issue of executive privilege soon arose in a concrete context. Assistant Attorney General Henry Petersen refused to discuss with the Special Prosecutor the exact content of conversations that he had had with the President, on the grounds that the conversations were perhaps subject to attorney-client privilege. Cox requested that Buzhardt determine whether the President would assert any "claim of legal privilege or other confidential relationship" that would prevent Petersen or former Attorney General Richard Kleindienst from fully disclosing their relevant conversations with him. In addition, Cox requested access to the tape recording of an April 15 conversation between the President and former White House counsel John Dean; evidence indicated its prime relevance to the cover-up investigation. In the next few days Cox also made requests for: (a) an inventory of the files of 12 Nixon aides and Administration officials; (b) all logs and diaries reflecting meetings and telephone calls between the President and 15 specified individuals; and (c) a letter explaining the administrative organization and procedures of the White House and listing the names of staff members of key Nixon aides.

Buzhardt responded with President Nixon's view that all of his discussions with Petersen and Kleindienst were within "both executive privilege and the attorney-client privilege," but said that the President had decided to waive all applicable privileges as to these discussions. With respect to the conversation between the President and Dean on April 15, Buzhardt stated that the President, when he had offered that tape to Petersen, had been referring only to the President's dictation of his own recollections of the conversation. Buzhardt's response concluded that "it would, of course, not be appropriate to produce that tape."

In responding to Buzhardt on June 20, Cox objected on two grounds to the President's denial of the tape recording of his recollections: first, since the President had offered to allow Petersen to listen to the tape, there could be no proper reason for withholding it from the Special Prosecutor who had assumed control of the Watergate investigation; second, the conversation was "critically important" to the task of untangling the complicated allegations about an attempt to cover up responsibility for the Watergate break-in. As Cox put it:

> In this case the witness is the President. Whatever may be the power of the Judicial Branch to subpoena him, it is certainly appropriate to obtain information from the President in ways less likely to interfere with the performance of his high responsibilities; and it is for this reason that I have thus far confined myself to a request for his recorded recollection [and not made a request for his personal testimony]. If the President wants the full facts developed without fear or favor—as I assume must be the case—then surely he must be willing for us to have such potentially important information without argument about any privilege he might theoretically assert.

During the next two weeks Cox also requested access to the "ITT" file maintained by Fred Fielding, one of Mr Dean's assistants.

By this time the White House had produced some documents in response to earlier requests. On June 22, WSPF received a list of Petersen's and Attorney General John Mitchell's meetings and telephone calls with the President. A week later, another letter explained the White House staff organization and enclosed a list of the staff members of various key personnel. In addition, WSPF received a copy of the list kept by Rose Mary Woods, the President's secretary, of pre-April 7, 1972, cash contributors to the Nixon campaign. There was no response, however, to Cox's request for inventories of White House files related to Watergate, the Fielding ITT file, or the President's taped recollections of his April 15 meeting with Dean. Nor was there any response to Cox's request of June 27 that the President provide a detailed written narrative responding to Dean's Senate Select Committee testimony.

Early in July, the office, in suggesting the need for delay in the Watergate civil suits, represented in court its intention to bring an indictment in the Watergate case no later than September. Nevertheless, a thorough investigation required access to additional White House files. On July 10, Cox wrote Buzhardt that "the delay [in responding to our requests] is now hampering our investigation of possible criminal offenses by high Government officials." Reminding Buzhardt that he had been "very patient—perhaps too patient—in seeking voluntary cooperation," Cox stated that he knew of no privilege that "would entitle the President to withhold documentary evidence of criminal misconduct on the part of Government employees or the White House staff." He warned that assertion of a privilege is "bound to be damaging to the President personally and to the office of the Presidency." Cox told the White House in unequivocal terms:

> I have repeatedly given public assurance that I would report upon any difficulty encountered in obtaining from the White House all information material to our investigation. I am reluctant either to take that course or to seek legal process before the opportunities for cooperation have been exhausted. Further delay would be so prejudicial to our work, however, that I must insist upon a prompt, categorical response to each of my prior requests and to the other requests for specific papers that I shall undoubtedly have occasion to make (including my letter of today's date).

As the letter indicated, Cox also made a request on the same date for additional information from the White House:

(1) Logs showing telephone conversations and meetings on July 5 and 6, 1972, between the President and Clark MacGregor;

(2) Copies of "political matters memoranda" from Gordon Strachan to H. R. Haldeman, two former White House aides;

(3) A copy of Dean's "miscellaneous intelligence" file;

(4) A copy of the logs showing the specific items from the files that had been copied by former White House staff members after April 30, 1973; and

(5) Copies of any records of items inserted into the White House files by former White House aides John Ehrlichman or David Young after April 30, 1973.

The White House responded on July 21. Expressing "great regret" for the delays, the President's attorney claimed that his office had been extremely busy with the Senate Select Committee hearings and subpoenas in civil actions and that the requests of the Special Prosecutor raised questions that had to be resolved by the President. Citing the President's international obligations and recent poor health, Buzhardt promised an early response to Cox's letter, but cautioned that "obtaining a decision from the President on sensitive questions that only he can decide is often not a speedy process."

Buzhardt's letter must be read in the context of the events that preceded it, beginning with testimony of Alexander Butterfield.

Grand jury subpoena duces tecum

On July 16, Alexander Butterfield, previously the President's staff secretary, told the Senate Select Committee that an automatic tape recording system had been installed in the President's White House and Executive Office Building offices in early 1971. According to Butterfield, this system was capable of recording automatically all telephone conversations and meetings in either office.

The significance of the President's recording system was immediately apparent. John Dean had testified that a number of his meetings with the President had implicated the President and his high aides in the Watergate cover-up. The recordings could provide invaluable corroboration for Dean's description of the meetings, as well as support his credibility on other aspects of his testimony, or they could show that his statements had been untrue.

The Special Prosecutor was faced with two concerns in determining how to proceed. First, although Cox was generally optimistic that President Nixon, like all his predecessors in office, would abide by any final court determination, he was anxious to avoid a possible constitutional confrontation between the judicial and executive branches if the President were to disobey a court order to produce the recordings. Second, Cox was concerned that enforcement proceedings necessarily would involve substantial delays in the investigation.

Despite these concerns, Cox concluded that WSPF could not proceed with the Watergate investigation without taking all possible steps to secure evidence that could be so important in determining responsibility for the Watergate cover-up.

Once he had decided to make a request for the recordings, Cox had to choose the conversations most essential to the investigation. A judicial decision would depend heavily on a balance between the need for confidentiality in deliberations of the Executive Branch and the need of the judicial process for evidence material to a criminal investigation and prosecution. Cox, therefore, chose the conversations that appeared essential to determining the truth or falsity of Dean's allegations before the Senate Select Committee. The tapes of the actual conversations would be crucial to the resolution of the grand jury's investigation. In addition, Cox picked those meetings which, from the available circumstantial evidence, would reveal the formation of any conspiracy—these included meetings of the President with Ehrlichman and Haldeman shortly after the break-in, one of the first conversations between the President and Mitchell after the break-in, and the meeting between the President and Mitchell on the day preceding Mitchell's resignation as director of CRP.

On July 18, Cox wrote to Buzhardt requesting access to the tape recordings of nine specified conversations. He emphasized "three essential aspects" of the request: first, the materiality of the recordings to the investigation of serious criminal misconduct; second, the lack of any separation of powers issue because the request was being made by a prosecutor within the executive branch, and not, for example, by the Senate Select Committee; and third, the confidentiality that attached to grand jury proceedings.

On July 23, Charles Alan Wright responded with the President's instructions that it would not be possible to make available the requested recordings, for reasons similar to those stated to Senator Ervin in denying a Senate Select Committee request. In addition, Wright argued that as part of the executive branch, the Special Prosecutor was subject to the direction of the President or the Attorney General and could not have access to Presidential papers unless the President saw fit to grant access. He argued:

> It is for the President, and only for the President, to weigh whether the incremental advantage that these tapes would give you in criminal proceedings justifies the serious and lasting hurt that disclosure of them would do to the confidentiality that is imperative to the effective functioning of the Presidency. In this instance the President has concluded that it would not serve the public interest to make the tapes available.

In a letter to Senator Ervin written the same day, the President indicated that "[if] release of the tapes would settle the central questions at issue in the Watergate inquiries, then their disclosure might serve a substantial public interest that would have to be weighed very heavily against the negatives of disclosure." He claimed that the tapes "would not finally settle the central issues," but that he had personally listened to a number of the tapes and they were "entirely consistent with what I know to be the truth and what I have stated to be the truth."

Upon receiving Wright's response, Cox announced at a press conference that he immediately would seek subpoenas to obtain the recordings. A subpoena returnable on July 26 was served immediately on the President's counsel.[1]

On July 25, the President wrote to Chief Judge Sirica and refused to comply with Cox's subpoena. He said he was following the example of predecessors who had "consistently adhered to the position that the President is not subject to compulsory process from the courts," and stated that it would be "inconsistent with the public interest and with the constitutional position of the Presidency to make available recordings of meetings and telephone conversations in which I was a participant."[2]

---

1. In addition to the tapes and related notes and memoranda, the subpoena called for the original of a memorandum on the termination of E. Howard Hunt as a White House consultant (a copy previously had been given to the FBI) and the "Political Matters Memoranda" prepared for Haldeman by Strachan. Cox believed that neither item was subject even to an arguable claim of privilege.

2. Nevertheless, he stated that, like his predecessors, he would voluntarily make available relevant material where that would not be "inconsistent with the public interest." He wrote that he was "voluntarily transmitting for the use of the grand jury" the memorandum on Hunt's termination and Strachan's Political Matters Memoranda. (The Hunt termination memorandum was enclosed with the letter, but the Political Matters Memoranda were not. They were not made available to the Special Prosecutor until September.)

The next morning, Cox explained to the grand jurors the President's refusal to comply with the subpoena and sought the grand jury's authorization to request an order from Chief Judge Sirica compelling the production of the tapes. Upon the unanimous vote to the grand jurors, the Special Prosecutor filed a petition for an order directing the President to show cause why the subpoenaed materials should not be produced. In the petition, the Special Prosecutor claimed that the grand jury had an enforceable right to access to the recordings, which were relevant and important to its investigations, and that the President, in a public statement on May 22, 1973, had waived any claim of executive privilege. (This statement authorized his aides to testify about Watergate before the Senate Select Committee.) Finally, the petition argued that it was the responsibility of the courts, and not the exclusive prerogative of the President, to determine whether a claim of privilege to withhold evidence from the courts was valid. After polling the grand jurors in open court and determining that it was their wish that the subpoena be enforced, Chief Judge Sirica signed the order to show cause, returnable on August 7.

On the return date, President Nixon filed a special appearance in which he contended that the order should be vacated because the court lacked jurisdiction to compel the President to comply with a subpoena.[3] The accompanying brief argued that compelled disclosure of the recordings not only would result in "severe and irreparable" damage "to the institution of the Presidency," but also would violate the constitutional doctrine of the separation of powers.

---

3. A special appearance permits a party to argue that the court lacks jurisdiction without submitting to the court's jurisdiction by the very fact of appearing.

The Special Prosecutor replied to this brief on August 13, arguing that the courts, as the historic arbiters of the Constitution, have the final authority to determine whether the executive can be required to produce evidence for use in a judicial proceeding and that the President is not absolutely immune from orders requiring him to comply with constitutional duties, including the production of unprivileged evidence. Acknowledging that the courts had recognized a qualified privilege in the interest of promoting candid policy discussions among executive officials, the Special Prosecutor contended that the privilege did not apply where there was reason to believe that the discussions may have involved criminal wrongdoing, and that, under the circumstances, the need of the grand jury for the subpoenaed recordings outweighed the public interest served by the confidentiality of the executive deliberations. Finally, the Special Prosecutor argued that any privilege attaching to the particular recordings had been waived by the President's consent to other disclosures of their content.

In his reply brief, the President claimed for the first time in court that he had ultimate responsibility for the prosecution of criminal cases and thus had ultimate control of what evidence would be produced for a criminal proceeding by the United States. The Special Prosecutor responded that the evidence was being sought by the grand jury, that the grand jury had independent authority to seek evidence wherever it might be, that the grand jury was not subject to the unfettered control of the executive branch, and that, in seeking enforcement of the subpoena, the Special Prosecutor was acting as the attorney of the grand jury and not merely as a subordinate member of the executive branch.

The issues were argued on August 22, 1973, before Chief Judge Sirica. The arguments were essentially those set forth in the briefs, with one notable exception. In his rebuttal argument, Wright stated that the President had told him that one of the subpoenaed tapes contained "national security material so highly sensitive" that the President could not even "hint" to Wright, who had a top secret clearance, the nature of the information.[4]

On August 29, 1973, Chief Judge Sirica ruled that the courts, and not the President, must make the ultimate determination of the validity and scope of any privilege asserted to bar them from obtaining evidence relevant to the proceedings and that they have the power to order a President to comply with a grand jury subpoena calling for unprivileged evidence in his possession. Although the Judge emphasized the need of the grand jury, he seemed to suggest that the privilege would yield only with respect to those conversations that did not occur pursuant to the President's exercise of his duty "to take care that the laws be faithfully executed," that is, those conversations that on their face revealed a criminal conspiracy. Clearly, mere relevance to Watergate was not the test. The judge ordered the President to produce the subpoenaed materials for court inspection, but stayed his order for five days to permit the President to seek appellate review.

Without awaiting the formal filing of papers, the Court of Appeals informally indicated to the parties that if review were sought the Court would hear oral arguments on September 11, using the briefs in the district court and any supplemental briefs the parties wished to file on September 10. Although objecting to the expeditious schedule, the President, after both noting an appeal and filing a petition for a writ of mandamus, filed a new brief on the Court of Appeals developing at greater length the

---

4. When the recordings eventually were produced, no claim relating to national security was made, and it soon became apparent that the tapes did not include any classified information.

issues that he had raised in the district court. The Special Prosecutor also petitioned the Court of Appeals for review, arguing that the inspection by Chief Judge Sirica was unnecessary because no valid claim of executive privilege could exist for any conversations actually relevant to the grand jury's proceedings. Alternatively, the Special Prosecutor asked the Court of Appeals to specify the particular standards that should govern the judge's inspection and argued that informed determinations of relevance could be made only with the Special Prosecutor's participation in the review.

On September 13, two days after oral argument, the Court of Appeals directed the parties to explore the possibility of reaching an agreement on voluntary submission of certain portions of the subpoenaed recordings to the grand jury. As the Court of Appeals stated:

> [I]f the President and the Special Prosecutor agree as to the material needed for the grand jury's functioning, the national interest will be served. At the same time, neither the President nor the Special Prosecutor would in any way have surrendered or subverted the principles for which they have contended.

After initial discussions, the Special Prosecutor submitted to the President's counsel a proposal that called for preparation of copies of the tapes with omissions of any portions not related to matters within the Special Prosecutor's jurisdiction; verification by a mutually acceptable person of the fact that the guidelines for omission had been accurately applied; and finality of the reviewer's determination. Before submission to the grand jury, the Special Prosecutor and counsel for the President would review the copies in an endeavor to agree upon the excision of any portion that was not material to the grand jury's investigation. Most important from the Special Prosecutor's viewpoint, the proposal included procedures for reviewing tapes that the Special Prosecutor might request in the future, either for the Watergate cover-up investigation or other grand jury investigations. A favorable court ruling at that time would have governed future requests, and if the Special Prosecutor were to forego final court resolution—after nearly two months of litigation—it was essential not to have to start from the beginning again if there should be another impasse over access. The proposal was unacceptable to the White House, however, and on September 20 both parties advised the Court that their discussions had been unsuccessful.

On October 12, the Court of Appeals, *en banc*, issued its decision rejecting the President's claims. The Court first decided that a President is not immune from judicial orders requiring the production of evidence for judicial proceedings. According to the Court, "sovereignty remains at all times with the people, and they do not forfeit through elections the right to have the law construed against and applied to every citizen." Citing the long-standing principle that the grand jury has a right to every person's evidence, the Court then held that executive privilege is not absolute, but must be balanced against other values. In this case, the Court ruled, the compelling need demonstrated by the grand jury outweighed the need of the executive branch to maintain the confidentiality of the particular conversations. In this regard the Court considered it important that public testimony concerning the conversations had substantially diminished any interest in maintaining further confidentiality. Finally the Court emphasized that the standard for court screening of the tapes was only to be one of relevance to the grand jury's proceedings, and not whether the President, in participating in the conversation, was engaging in his constitutional duties. The Court stayed its order for five days to permit the President to seek review in the Supreme Court.

The Stennis compromise and the dismissal of Cox

On the Friday afternoon of the Court of Appeals decision, but before it had been announced, Cox met with Attorney General Richardson about an unrelated matter. During the meeting, Richardson philosophized about the need for a public official to know when to take a stand on a matter of principle. The following Monday, during another meeting hastily called by the Attorney General, Richardson stated that "serious consequences" might ensue if Cox were not to agree to a compromise on the tapes by the close of business Friday, October 19, the date on which the President was due to file his petition for review by the Supreme Court. Although Cox expressed great reservations about negotiating under a deadline, and argued that there was no need to complete the negotiations so rapidly, he agreed to explore the possibility of a compromise.

After another meeting with Richardson on Tuesday the 16th, when Cox suggested that it would be best if Richardson were to put his proposal in writing, Richardson the next day delivered to Cox a document entitled "A Proposal." The stated objective was to provide "a means of furnishing to the court and grand jury a complete and accurate record of the content of the tapes subpoenaed by the Special Prosecutor insofar as the conversations recorded in those tapes in any way relate to the Watergate break-in and the cover-up of the break-in." The proposal provided that the President would select an individual to verify transcripts previously prepared by the White House—transcripts that would be verbatim, but would omit continuous portions unrelated to Watergate and would be in the "third person." The verifier would be permitted to paraphrase language "whose use in its original form would in his judgment be embarrassing to the President" and, in the interests of national security, to omit sections related to the national defense or foreign relations. Finally, the proposal would require the Special Prosecutor to join with counsel for the President in urging the Court to accept the verified transcripts as full and accurate records of all pertinent portions of the tapes "for all purposes for which access to those tapes might thereafter be sought by or on behalf of any person having standing to obtain such access."

Cox responded to Richardson on Thursday the 18th in a document entitled "Comments on 'A Proposal.'" He stated his willingness to accept the "essential idea of establishing impartial, but non-judicial means for providing the Special Prosecutor and grand jury with an accurate record of the contents of the tapes without [the Special Prosecutor's] participation," but listing eleven specific comments that struck him as "highly important," including the following:

(1) The public cannot be fairly asked to confide so difficult and responsible a task to any *one* man operating in secrecy, consulting only with the White House. Nor should we be put in the position of accepting any choice made unilaterally.

(2) The stated objective of the proposal is too narrow. It should include providing evidence that in any way relates to other possible criminal activity under the jurisdiction of this office.

(3) I do not understand the implications of saying that the "verbatim transcript ... would be in the third person." I do assume that the names of all speakers, of all persons addressed by name or tone, and of all persons mentioned would be included.

(4) A "transcript" prepared in the manner projected might be enough for investigation by the Special Prosecutor

and the grand jury. If we accept such a "transcript" we would try to get it accepted by the courts (as you suggest). There must also be assurance, however, that if the indictments are returned, if evidence concerning any of the nine conversations would, in our judgment, be important at the trial, and if the court will not accept our "transcript" then the evidence will be furnished to the prosecution in whatever form the trial court rules is necessary for admissibility (including as much of the original tape as the court requires). Similarly, if the court rules that a tape or any portion must be furnished to a defendant or the case will be dismissed, then the tape must be supplied.

(5) The narrow scope of the proposal is a grave defect, because it would not serve the function of court decision in establishing the Special Prosecutor's entitlement to other evidence. We have long pending requests for many specific documents. The proposal also leaves half a lawsuit hanging (i.e., the subpoenaed papers). Some method of resolving these problems is required.

(6) The Watergate Special Prosecution Force was established because of a widely felt need to create an independent office that would objectively and forthrightly pursue the *prima facie* showing of criminality by high Government officials. You appointed me, and I have pledged that I would not be turned aside. Any solution I can accept must be such as to command conviction that I am adhering to that pledge.

Later that night, Wright telephoned Cox to inform him that certain of his comments were unacceptable. Cox realized that a confrontation was inevitable and believed that all communications should be in writing so that there would be a record of each side's position. He asked Wright to address a letter stating the President's response to the comment that Cox had delivered to Richardson. Cox promised a prompt reply.

Early on Friday morning, October 19, Wright's letter was delivered. Briefly, it stated that the "very reasonable proposal that the Attorney General put to you, at the instance of the President," was intended to provide information necessary to the grand jury and to "put to rest any possible thought that the President might himself have been involved in the Watergate break-in or cover-up." Wright stated the President's belief that the proposal would serve the national interest, but that four of Mr Cox's comments "depart so far from that proposal and the purpose for which it was made that we could not accede to them in any form." The four unacceptable comments included the objection to one person reviewing the tapes and to that person being selected solely by the White House; the suggestion that the reviewers be appointed "special masters" and thus accountable to the court rather than the parties; the demand that the tapes be made available if a court required; and the demand that the proposal also be applied to pending and future requests. Finally, Wright said:

> If you think that there is any purpose in our talking further, my associates and I stand ready to do so. If not, we will have to follow the course of action that we think in the best interest of the country.

Cox replied as requested by 10:00 that morning, setting forth his understanding of the conversation the preceding evening—that is, that Wright had stated that there was no point in continuing conversations in an effort to reach a "reasonable out of court accommodation" unless Cox accepted categorically the President's position with respect to certain key provisions. In addition to stating that the President already had selected the only person he would consider acceptable to review the tapes, that there could not be a special master under a court order, and that no portion of the tapes themselves would be provided under any circumstances, Wright had indicated that Cox would have to agree not to subpoena any other White House tapes, papers, or documents, no matter how relevant to criminal wrong-doing by White House officials. In conclusion, Cox wrote:

> I have a strong desire to avoid any form of confrontation, but I could not conscientiously agree to your stipulations without unfaithfulness to the pledges which I gave the Senate prior to my appointment. It is enough to point out that the fourth stipulation would require me to forego further legal challenge to claims of executive privilege. I categorically assured the Senate Judiciary Committee that I would challenge such claims so far as the law permitted. The Attorney General was confirmed on the strength of that assurance. I cannot break my promise now.

Wright responded that "further discussions between us seeking to resolve this matter by compromise would be futile, ... we will be forced to take the actions that the President deems appropriate in the circumstances." He added that he wished to clear up two points "in the inter-est of historical accuracy, in the unhappy event that our correspondence should see the light of day." First, he said that the issue of eventual availability of the tapes was a matter open to negotiation, but that the President would not give any advance commitment; second, the Special Prosecutor would be barred only from subpoenaing "pri-vate Presidential papers and meetings," not the great mass of White House documents with which the President was not personally involved.

That night, October 19, President Nixon issued a state-ment setting forth the so-called "Stennis compromise" and announcing his decision not to seek Supreme Court review of the Court of Appeals decision. The "Stennis compromise," which accorded with the basic outlines of the Richardson proposal of Wednesday morning, provided that Senator John Stennis would review the tapes to verify the White House transcripts and that the President would make available to Judge Sirica, as well as to the Senate Select Committee, the Watergate-related portions of the authenticated transcripts.

At the same time, the President delivered a letter to Attorney General Richardson directing him to instruct Cox "to make no further attempts by judicial process to obtain tapes, notes, or memoranda of presidential conversations." He added that he regretted "the necessity of intruding, to this very limited extent, on the independence that I promised you with regard to Watergate when I announced your appointment. This would not have been necessary if the Special Prosecutor had agreed to the very reasonable proposal you made to him this week." Richardson told Cox about the letter, but emphasized that he was not delivering the instructions that the President had directed him to give.

Cox hurriedly prepared a brief statement which he read to the press that evening. Accusing the President of "refusing to comply with the court decrees," Cox stated that he would challenge the Stennis compromise in court. He added that he could not "violate" his promise to the Senate and the country to invoke judicial process "to challenge exaggerated claims of executive privilege." In an hour-long press conference held at noon the following day, October 20, Cox elaborated on his belief that acceptance of the President's directions would defeat the fair administration of criminal justice by compromising the Special Prosecutor's independence and insulating the President from the courts.

The dismissal of Cox and related events are described elsewhere in this report. Public reaction played a substantial part in the President's later decision to comply in full with the court order and to abandon the Stennis plan. When Wright appeared before Judge Sirica on Tuesday, October 23, he announced that because of "the events of the week-end," the President had decided to abide by the Court of Appeals ruling.

Production of the subpoenaed materials and the tapes hearings

In the week that followed the President's reversal, the parties agreed on procedures and a timetable for production of the subpoenaed tapes and related materials. Chief Judge Sirica announced on October 30 that White House counsel would submit the tapes with an accompanying analysis indicating the portions of the recordings that did not relate to Watergate and thus were still privileged. Judge Sirica then would review each recording, and give the grand jury all portions relevant to its investigation.[5]

On October 31, however, Buzhardt reported to the Court that recordings of the telephone call from Mitchell to President Nixon on June 20, 1972, and the meeting between President Nixon and Dean on April 15, 1973, did not exist. As Buzhardt later explained, the June 20 telephone

---

5. The only recording that White House counsel asserted was totally unrelated to Watergate was the recording of the June 30, 1972, meeting between President Nixon and Mitchell. After reviewing the recording and consulting with the Special Prosecutor, the judge determined that two brief passages should be submitted to the grand jury. White House counsel also asserted privilege with respect to the final portion of the September 15, 1972, meeting between President Nixon and Haldeman. The judge upheld the claim, but upon motion of the Special Prosecutor later released the portion to a different grand jury in connection with the investigation into alleged White House misuse of the Internal Revenue Service.

call, received by the President in the residence area of the White House, had not been recorded, and the Dean meeting was not recorded because the tape had run out earlier on the busy Sunday of April 15.

After conferring with the parties, Chief Judge Sirica decided to hold hearings to explore how the taping system had been installed and maintained, how the tapes were stored, who had access to them, and why the June 20 call and April 15 meeting had not been recorded. These hearings, primarily with the testimony of Secret Service agents and White House aides who had been responsible for the system, lasted approximately two weeks and then were recessed.

On November 21, Buzhardt disclosed that 18½ minutes of the recording of the June 20, 1972, meeting between President Nixon and Haldeman had been obliterated.[6] Only a buzzing sound could be heard. Haldeman's notes of the meeting confirmed that the erased portion concerned Watergate. Chief Judge Sirica reconvened the tapes hearings, with testimony from Woods (who admitted accidentally erasing a short segment of the 18½ minutes), White House chief of staff General Alexander Haig, Buzhardt, and White House aide Stephen Bull. The Court, with the consent of the parties, also appointed a six-member panel of experts to test and analyze the tapes. Upon conclusion of hearings and receipt of the experts' report, Chief Judge Sirica referred the record of the proceedings to the grand jury for its consideration. (This investigation is described in the previous chapter of this report.)

---

6. Subsequently, White House counsel revealed the existence of much shorter gaps in the President's taped recollections of his June 20 telephone call with Mitchell and his March 21, 1973 meeting with Haldeman and Dean.

Renewed requests for tapes and documents

One of the principal issues during the period between Cox's dismissal and the appointment of Special Prosecutor Jaworski was whether the officials of the Department, including Acting Attorney General Bork and Assistant Attorney General Petersen, who had taken charge of the Special Prosecutor's investigations, would stand behind the staff in seeking evidentiary material in the control of the President. Although Cox had refrained from making many requests pending the outcome of the tapes litigation, three of WSPF's recent letters requesting documents had not been answered. On August 23, Cox had written to Buzhardt requesting a series of records relating to the office's investigation of the "Plumbers" break-in at the office of Dr Lewis Fielding, Daniel Ellsberg's former psychiatrist. Four days later he had requested records relating to the investigation of the wiretap of journalist Joseph Kraft, and on October 10 he had requested documents relating to the May 3, 1972, assault on antiwar demonstrators on the Capitol steps. The office had not received a definitive response to any of these requests, nor to other requests that had been made long before the subpoena for the Presidential tapes had been served.

Petersen agreed to renew each of the requests after reviewing WSPF's ongoing investigations with individual task force leaders and determining that there was "a clear and immediate need for the production of the documents and other records." On November 1, he addressed a letter to Buzhardt asking for quick production of the logs of meetings between ten individuals and the President, a request that had been outstanding since June, and reiterating the requests of August and October relating to the Fielding break-in, the Kraft wiretap, and the May 3 assault. The next day he requested all records relating to the 1970 "Townhouse" operation—a funding operation for congressional candidates—in connection with an investigation into possible violations of the Federal Corrupt Practices Act.

On November 5, Leon Jaworski was sworn in as the second Special Prosecutor with assurances of full cooperation from the White House. On November 7, after an initial round of briefings on the status of all investigations, Jaworski made his first request for materials: copies of recordings of conversations between the President and Ehrlichman, Mitchell and Kleindienst on April 19 and 20, 1971, relating to the International Telephone and Telegraph Corporation ("ITT"). On the following day, he renewed the earlier requests for materials in the "Plumbers" files, and on November 15, he requested copies of recordings of conversations between the President and his former assistant Charles Colson in early January 1973 for use in the Watergate investigation. In each of his letters, Jaworski asked for an early response.

Jaworski had met with Buzhardt and General Alexander Haig, the President's chief of staff, on November 13, in part to discuss his recent requests for tape recordings and to stress the grand juries' need for prompt responses. They assured Jaworski that cooperation would be forthcoming. Then, on November 19, Jaworski wrote to Buzhardt asking him to respond to the outstanding requests made before the dismissal of Cox and the more recent requests made by Petersen. He stated that failure to respond was "delaying and in some instances impeding our investigations." Jaworski made it clear that he would not tolerate any delays like those experienced by Cox:

> In light of past experience, I believe it entirely appropriate to ask you to acknowledge each of these requests and explain your current position. As to those materials you intend to produce, please let us know when you expect to

produce them. If you must review certain materials, please
let us know when you will review them and when we can
expect a definitive response. Finally, if there are any
materials you do not plan to produce in response to our
requests, please identify them and inform us why you are
not producing them.

On November 24, Jaworski received an omnibus response
from Buzhardt on outstanding requests. He stated that
although searches for requested recordings require "enormous expenditures of time," the recordings that could be
located would be provided. He then responded specifically
to each request for documents, enclosing the documents
that could be found and stating which could not. In short,
Buzhardt's letter constituted a seemingly favorable
response to many WSPF requests, but as Jaworski indicated
in his reply of November 30, it merely acknowledged the
existence of other requests, particularly in the Watergate
and "Plumbers" areas, without indicating whether they
would be met. Jaworski also protested the intimation in
Buzhardt's letter that the Special Prosecutor's office had
been less than cooperative in understanding the attendant
delays, and concluded "that if our several requests are
treated in the light of the White House's announced readi-
ness to extend full cooperation—and we have no reason to
believe otherwise—unequivocal response to our remaining
requests should be forthcoming in another week or ten
days."

In the following week the office renewed the request
for Townhouse documents, only a few of which had been
provided; made an extensive request for records relating
to the investigation of dairy industry contributions; and
renewed the request in more detailed form for materials
in the "Plumbers" files. On December 6, Jaworski also
wrote to Haig, complaining that over three weeks had

elapsed since their meeting on November 13 when Haig and Buzhardt had promised cooperation. Although certain documents had been provided on November 24, no tapes had been produced. Stressing the immediate need for delivery of the requested tapes and other materials, including the "Plumbers" files and files relating to contributions by the dairy industry, Jaworski warned that a subpoena would be issued early the next week if necessary.

The next day, Jaworski met with Haig and Buzhardt, and on December 8, the White House produced eight of the requested recordings. These related to the ITT investigation, the dairy industry investigation, the "Plumbers," and the Watergate investigation. The White House claimed that the other requested conversations had not been recorded, either because they had taken place outside of the White House or because the telephone conversations were on lines that were not subject to the recording system. Finally, Haig and Buzhardt maintained that still other conversations were irrelevant to the investigations; it was agreed, however, that Jaworski would be allowed to review them, and one which Jaworski determined to be relevant was later produced. The White House also agreed to allow a member of the staff to review the files of the "Plumbers" unit.

During his appearance at the Senate Judiciary Committee's confirmation hearings on the nomination of William Saxbe to be Attorney General, Jaworski had assured the Committee that he would report at an appropriate time on the status of the office's efforts to obtain evidence from the White House. On December 13, in a letter to Committee Chairman James Eastland, Jaworski reported "significant cooperation from the White House" and stated that he hoped for a "mutually satisfactory resolution" of pending requests.

Access after the commencement of the impeachment inquiry

In January of 1974, James D. St Clair was appointed as the President's chief counsel for "Watergate"-related matters. By that time, the impeachment inquiry by the House Judiciary Committee had begun in earnest. It was clear from the outset that the arrival of St Clair would occasion further delays in obtaining information from the White House. St Clair needed time to acquaint himself not only with "Watergate" in general and the President's potential liability in any area of the Special Prosecutor's requests, but also with prior relationships and understandings between WSPF and the White House. The Special Prosecutor believed it essential to renew the requests that were outstanding and to emphasize to St Clair that inordinate delays would be intolerable. Accordingly, on January 8, Deputy Special Prosecutor Henry Ruth addressed a letter to St Clair asking for specified items relating to the office's investigation of the dairy industry.[7] The next day, Jaworski requested recordings of 25 meetings or telephone conversations relating to the Watergate cover-up investigation, explaining that these tapes were necessary to permit as full an investigation as possible before any indictments were returned.

On January 22, Jaworski met with St Clair, who indicated that the President would not make a decision with respect to the January 9 requests until the Special Prosecutor provided a justification for each of the requested recordings. That same day, although stating that he did not believe that a showing of "particularized need" was required for each conversation, Jaworski sent St Clair an explanation of the importance of each conversation to the Watergate investigation.

---

7. Jaworski had recused himself from all matters regarding this investigation.

At the same meeting, Jaworski and St Clair also discussed the possibility of obtaining the President's testimony before the grand jury. St Clair suggested that Jaworski consider propounding written interrogatories to the President, with the possibility of Jaworski conducting a personal interview after the President answered the interrogatories. Jaworski countered with the suggestion that the grand jury come to the White House, an alternative that St Clair said would be unacceptable. The following day, Jaworski wrote St Clair that written interrogatories generally are not a useful or effective method for obtaining a person's testimony. But, in order to consider fully the St Clair proposal, Jaworski asked that St Clair determine whether the President would answer under oath, how long it would take the President to provide answers, whether tapes and documents relevant to the answers would be provided, and who, in addition to the Special Prosecutor, would be permitted to interview the President after the interrogatories were answered. On January 25, St Clair responded that he was prepared to recommend to the President that the answers to the interrogatories be given under oath, but that in the light of the materials already provided to the Special Prosecutor, it would not be suitable to provide further tapes and documents. He also indicated that only Jaworski should conduct the interview.

As to the January 9 request for Watergate-related tapes, St Clair claimed that under the Court of Appeals decision of October 12, 1973, in *Nixon* v. *Sirica*, WSPF had to show a "uniquely powerful" need for the tapes and that they constituted "evidence for which no effective substitute is available." The tapes requested, he contended, were merely cumulative of the testimony of witnesses before the Senate Select Committee and thus could serve only as corroboration for the grand jury. Although he concluded that the January 22 justifications for Watergate tapes did not meet these requirements, he stated that no final decision had been made as to whether the material called for would be produced voluntarily and promised a definitive response early the next week.

During the first month after St Clair arrived, the only items produced were those that had been promised during 1973. Each time items were delivered to the Special Prosecutor they were accompanied by a letter stating that the materials were being furnished "solely for your use in presenting evidence to the grand jury." It became clear over the next weeks that St Clair was primarily concerned that evidence produced for the grand jury not subsequently be provided by WSPF to the House Judiciary Committee for use in its impeachment inquiry. Believing it necessary to clarify the status of the materials received, Jaworski wrote to St Clair on January 25, stating that the office would lay before the grand jury any relevant evidence bearing on matters within the Special Prosecutor's jurisdiction, but that it was necessarily implicit that, if the grand jury were to return indictments, any evidence provided to the office, whether under subpoena or voluntarily, could be used at any trials resulting from grand jury investigations.

On January 30 Jaworski again asked St Clair by letter for a response to WSPF's numerous outstanding requests.[8] That night, in his State of the Union Address, the President said that he had turned over all the evidence that the

---

8. These included: the January 9 request for tapes related to Watergate, the November 2 and December 3 requests for documents relating to the "Townhouse" operation, the December 3 request for records relating to the appointments of ambassadors, the August 27 request for records relating to the wiretap of Joseph Kraft, the December 18 request for Fred Fielding's records relating to IRS, the December 4 request for documents relating to ITT, the January 8 request for documents relating to the dairy industry, and the October 10 request for documents relating to the May 3, 1972 assault on demonstrators.

Special Prosecutor needed to complete his Watergate investigation. In a similar statement to the press outside the courthouse the next day, St Clair hinted that no more evidence would be forthcoming. Hoping to clarify the situation, Jaworski wrote to St Clair on February 1 asking whether it was then clear that the White House would not voluntarily produce any additional evidence. Three days later, St Clair responded: it was the President's view that he had furnished sufficient evidence to determine whether there was probable cause for returning indictments and that further production would only delay the investigations. He voiced the hope that some alternative means of furnishing needed information could be agreed upon to avoid "prolonged litigation." At the same time, St Clair indicated that he would have to review the requests for documents and that he would respond as soon as possible.

White House attention was then focused solely on the impeachment inquiry. Perhaps one of the most troubling points for the Special Prosecutor was the Administration's concerted attack on John Dean, an important witness in the Watergate investigation. In response to this attack, wherein Senate Minority Leader Hugh Scott and others had issued statements demeaning Dean's credibility, on February 3 Jaworski publicly stated his belief in Dean's veracity. Three days earlier WSPF had found it necessary to vouch for Dean's credibility in a court proceeding. On February 4, the day that St Clair indicated that no more tapes would be made available to the Special Prosecutor (tapes obviously critical to determining whether or not John Dean was telling the full truth), the White House press office released the following statement in St Clair's name:

> I have noted that the Special Prosecutor and members of
> his staff have seen to discuss in public their views regarding
> John Dean's veracity. I can say categorically, however, that

the tapes and other evidence furnished to the Special
Prosecutor—at least as far as the President is concerned—
do not support sworn statements before the Senate Select
Committee made by Mr Dean as to what the President
knew about Watergate, and especially when he knew it. The
evidence does support what the President has said on this
matter.

I do not intend, nor would it be appropriate for me, to
discuss the technical, legal issues of perjury. I suggest the
time and place for discussing such matters is in court, or
perhaps before the House Judiciary Committee, not in the
public media. For this reason, I do not believe it would be
appropriate to further discuss this matter at this time.

On February 8, Jaworski met with St Clair to discuss
the President's refusal to provide additional tapes. If the
President supplied the tapes already requested for the
Watergate grand jury investigation, St Clair asked, would
the Special Prosecutor agree not to request any further
tapes in connection with that investigation? Jaworski
responded in writing that he would be willing to forego
future requests for the grand jury investigation, if it was
understood that "this agreement would not foreclose further requests that may be occasioned by legitimate defense
demands or our trial preparation needs after indictment."

On February 13, St Clair responded that the President
had refused to reconsider his earlier decision to end his
cooperation, at least with regard to producing any tape
recordings of Presidential conversations. It was clear to
Jaworski that any voluntary cooperation was at an end, and,
in accordance with his obligation to report to the Senate
Judiciary Committee on the status of requests to the White
House for evidence, he wrote to Senator Eastland to out-
line the correspondence of the first week of February and
summarize the materials provided and refused by the White

House from the beginning of the Special Prosecutor's office to date. Jaworski added:

> Although it is true that the grand jury will be able to return indictments without the benefit of this material, the material is important to a complete and thorough investigation and may contain evidence necessary for any future trials.

At the same time, the Special Prosecutor decided that prolonged litigation to obtain more tapes for the grand jury would unduly delay the Watergate indictment. Accordingly, at his recommendation, the grand jury returned an indictment on March 1 in *United States* v. *Mitchell*, the Watergate cover-up case.[9]

Other grand jury investigations were also pending, and President Nixon also refused to turn over any documents or tapes for them. On February 27, St Clair wrote that because the President believed that the grand juries had sufficient evidence, he would not consent to provide any materials relating to "Townhouse," appointment of ambassadors, White House contacts with IRS, ITT, or the May 3 incident. As to "Townhouse," St Clair also challenged the Special Prosecutor's jurisdiction because the investigations involved the 1970 congressional elections. Jaworski responded immediately that he could not "imagine" how the White House knows whether the grand jury had been "furnished 'sufficient evidence' to render fair and thorough consideration to the question of returning indictments." He also challenged the assertion that he had no jurisdiction

---

9. Prior to ending its investigation, the grand jury invited President Nixon to testify. The President refused, on the grounds that it would be inappropriate for a President in light of the constitutional separation of powers to subject himself to questioning before the grand jury.

over the "Townhouse" matter. On March 2, St Clair "withdrew" his letter.

Although "Townhouse" documents were produced on March 14, it appeared that there would not be any significant voluntary cooperation in other areas. Accordingly, on that day Jaworski issued a subpoena on behalf of the grand jury for documents relating to the appointments and campaign contributions of four ambassadors. Shortly after the subpoena was served, St Clair requested an adjournment of the return date, and on March 29 the President began voluntary compliance.

At about the same time, the President produced a short portion of the recording of a meeting for use in former White House aide Dwight Chapin's perjury trial, but significant voluntary cooperation with WSPF then ceased. The President refused to permit the office to review the files of his former assistants Ehrlichman and Colson in connection with the upcoming Fielding break-in.[10] Furthermore despite an assurance on April 4 that the office would receive a prompt response to a modified and narrower request for tapes and documents relating to the dairy industry investigation, no response was forthcoming. Indeed, it was not until late June that St Clair informed WSPF that no tapes would be provided.

The Watergate trial subpoena duces tecum

On March 12, Jaworski wrote to St Clair requesting access to recordings believed important to preparation for the Watergate cover-up trial. Jaworski requested a response no later than March 19, so that any litigation necessary could

---

10. Later, when the White House refused to permit Ehrlichman access to the materials and a dismissal of the indictment was threatened, the White House modified its position to accommodate the minimum requirements set by the trial judge.

be initiated promptly in order to avoid any delay in the scheduled trial date of September 9. On March 22, St Clair responded that the request was under "active consideration." He added that the White House had received a similar request from the House Committee on the Judiciary, "the resolution of which will obviously bear on your request." During several meetings and telephone conversations with St Clair over the following days, it became clear that WSPF would receive only those materials that were to be made available to the House Committee.[11] According to St Clair, the President would not consider other requests until he had decided what to provide to the Committee. Moreover, St Clair would not specify what criteria would govern the President's response.

Thereafter, on April 11, Jaworski wrote to St Clair to inform him that he would seek a trial subpoena on April 16. In response, St Clair withdrew from earlier oral statements to Jaworski and wrote that the office's requests were not tied in the White House's view to those of the House Committee "other than in the practical sense that it is more expeditious to furnish the same material to you and to the House Committee at the same time." As to the criteria that would govern the President's response, he stated that the response would depend upon the evidence necessary to a successful prosecution. The President, he said, would have to balance this need against the public interest, having in mind the Court of Appeals' statement in *Nixon* v. *Sirica* that wholesale public access to executive deliberations would cripple the executive branch. St Clair also noted that

---

11. At the hearing before Judge Sirica on whether the Watergate grand jury report on President Nixon would be transmitted to the House Judiciary Committee, St Clair had informed the Court that the President would make available to the House all materials that had been provided to the Special Prosecutor.

because the grand jury had returned an indictment, he presumed there already was sufficient evidence to convict each of the defendants. Finally, he added that he was "somewhat at a loss to understand how you are in a position to assert that you need the materials requested since you do not know what is contained in the recordings in question."

On April 16, the Special Prosecutor filed a motion before Judge Sirica requesting that he issue a trial subpoena to the President for recordings of 64 specified conversations, stating that production was sought before trial in order to permit review and transcription of the recordings without necessitating a delay in the trial. The 64 recordings had been chosen by reviewing all the evidence then available to the Special Prosecutor including those conversations which could be specifically identified and which, because of either circumstantial evidence or available testimony,[12] the office had reason to believe would be relevant to proving the cover-up conspiracy. In addition, because the prosecutors knew they must counter the argument that the need for the recordings did not outweigh the interest in confidentiality of executive deliberations, they chose only those conversations that were "demonstrably important" to defining the extent of the conspiracy in terms of time, membership and objectives.

Judge Sirica issued a subpoena on April 18. On May 2, the return date, the President filed a special appearance and a motion to quash the subpoena. Although the President claimed no privilege with respect to the Watergate-related portions of the conversations for which he had provided

---

12. In some cases, there was testimony either before the grand jury or in other forums indicating that the conversation in question related to Watergate. In other cases, the Special Prosecutor judged from events either before or after the conversation in question that the conversation probably concerned Watergate.

transcripts to the House Judiciary Committee on April 30, he claimed executive privilege with respect to the remaining materials.[13] In his supporting memorandum, the President argued first that the Special Prosecutor had not made a sufficient showing that the items were relevant. Indeed, he argued that because the Special Prosecutor could not show exactly what was in the recordings, he could not establish their relevance to the trial. Next, the President contended that the Special Prosecutor's showing of need was insufficient. The President claimed that the need for evidence by a grand jury is much greater than that of a prosecutor in a post-indictment setting. Because the Special Prosecutor had sufficient evidence to make a *prima facie* showing of guilt against the persons indicted, the President argued, the items sought by the subpoena at best could be classified as "merely cumulative or corroborative— certainly not vital or particularly necessary." The President did indicate, however, that if any defendant could show that particular items were exculpatory as to him, the President would consider producing them.

WSPF knew that its legal position would be strongest if the Special Prosecutor disclosed to the Court that the grand jury had voted to authorize the Special Prosecutor to name President Nixon as an unindicted co-conspirator in the Watergate trial. The grand jury's finding was important because it formed a factual predicate for the legal argument that executive privilege did not apply to any conversations that occurred in the course of and in furtherance of a criminal conspiracy. The office believed that the public purpose underlying executive privilege—to promote bona fide governmental deliberations—could not support the shielding of alleged criminality. Disclosure of the grand

---

13. On April 30, the President submitted to the House Judiciary Committee transcripts of 43 Watergate-related conversations.

jury's finding was obviously a sensitive and grave matter, and Jaworski believed that he should advise St Clair and Haig that such a disclosure would be made in the event of further proceedings to enforce the subpoena. On Sunday, May 5, Jaworski informed them of the grand jury's finding and stated that unless there were voluntary compliance with the subpoena, at least with respect to 16 conversations regarded as essential to the prosecution, he would make the necessary use of the grand jury's finding to present the best legal arguments against the President's motion to quash. Haig and St Clair asked for additional time to consider the matter before the Special Prosecutor filed his response to the motion.

After listening to the conversations that Jaworski had identified as crucial, including meetings with Haldeman on June 23, 1972, the President decided not to comply in any respect with the subpoena. Accordingly, on May 6, the Special Prosecutor filed his response with the District Court. At the suggestion of the Special Prosecutor, the response, which included a statement of the grand jury's finding, was filed under seal, since Jaworski believed that in light of the pending impeachment inquiry, it would be extremely unfair to have the grand jury's finding made public at that time, unless that was necessary to the litigation. In addition to his legal memorandum, the Special Prosecutor filed a 49-page appendix detailing the relevance of each subpoenaed conversation. He argued that the available testimony about the conversations, as well as the circumstances surrounding each conversation, clearly supported a finding that each would be relevant to the trial and that the Court should not require a greater showing of relevance where the prosecutor in fact did not have access to the actual evidence. He then argued that no executive privilege was available because each of the participants in the conversation was a co-conspirator and each conversation occurred in the course of the conspiracy. Alternatively, he claimed that the need for the evidence, which related to aspects of the conspiracy for which no other reliable evidence was available, outweighed any interest in secrecy. The Special Prosecutor urged that the need for the evidence was even greater now than in the grand jury because the Government has at trial the burden of showing guilt beyond a reasonable doubt.

Finally, in addition to arguing that the numerous disclosures by the President about Watergate, including the transcripts provided to the House Judiciary Committee on April 30, waived any claim of executive privilege, the Special Prosecutor argued that it was essential to obtain the actual tapes of the conversations. Transcripts of the conversations would not suffice. To support this point he compared some of the transcripts submitted by the White House with those prepared by the WSPF for the grand jury. That comparison indicated material differences between the two sets of transcripts. Important portions had been deleted or marked as unintelligible in the White House transcripts.

In reply, the President filed a motion to expunge the grand jury's finding. He argued that the grand jury had no jurisdiction over the President—that the President could be subject only to impeachment for alleged wrongdoing and not to the criminal jurisdiction of the courts. The President for the first time also raised the argument that the court did not have jurisdiction over the dispute because it was "entirely intra-executive in nature."

The Special Prosecutor in turn filed a memorandum urging that while it was not necessary for the court to decide the difficult issue whether the grand jury could have indicted President Nixon, there was no question that the grand jury could find that the President was an unindicted co-conspirator. Noting that the Constitution did not confer any immunity on the President, the Special Prosecutor argued that, because the mere naming of the President as a co-conspirator does not have any practical consequences on the President's ability to perform his constitutional duties, the grand jury's finding did not violate the separation of powers doctrine. As to the issue of jurisdiction, he argued that there was in fact a case or controversy because, under the WSPF regulations that were binding upon the Department of Justice and the President, the Special Prosecutor had exclusive jurisdiction for conducting the prosecution of the Watergate case and was not subject to the direction of the President or Attorney General. Thus, the Special Prosecutor was not for these purposes a "subordinate" of the President. Jaworski emphasized that when he had been selected as Special Prosecutor, he had received repeated assurances from Bork, Saxbe, and Haig that his independence would not be interfered with. Finally, the Special Prosecutor urged the court to make all the proceedings public in view of the attack on his authority to seek and enforce the subpoena for Presidential conversations.

Judge Sirica issued his opinion and order enforcing the subpoena on May 20. At the outset, he held that as long as the regulations establishing the independence of the Special Prosecutor were in effect, the President's "attempt to abridge the Special Prosecutor's independence with the argument that he cannot seek evidence from the President by court process is a nullity and does not defeat the court's jurisdiction." Accepting WSPF's showing of relevance and admissibility, the court held that the demonstration of need was "sufficiently compelling to warrant judicial examination in chambers incident to weighing claims of privilege where the privilege has not been relinquished." Finally, as to the President's motion to expunge the grand jury's findings, Judge Sirica stated that he saw no need "to grant more extensive protective orders at this time or to expunge portions of the record. Matters sought to be expunged are relevant, for example, to a determination that the presumption of privilege is overcome." Judge Sirica ordered the President to submit the recordings to the court on or before May 31 but stayed his order until May 24 to permit the President to seek appellate review.

On May 24, the President sought review in the Court of Appeals. That same day, however, the Special Prosecutor filed a petition in the Supreme Court for direct review of Judge Sirica's order. Under Supreme Court rules, this procedure, which allows the Supreme Court to review a case before it is decided by the Court of Appeals, is reserved for cases of imperative public importance. As the Special Prosecutor represented in the petition, expedited consideration by the Supreme Court was important to permit the Watergate trial to proceed as quickly as possible. He estimated that if the Supreme Court were to wait until its October 1974 Term, there would be a delay of at least six months in the start of the trial. Moreover, he submitted that there was little need for a Court of Appeals decision, since that Court had considered the same constitutional issues in deciding the validity of the grand jury subpoena in *Nixon v. Sirica* the preceding October. The Special Prosecutor's petition presented five issues for review by the Court:

(1) Whether the President is subject to a judicial order directing compliance with the subpoena *duces tecum* issued on the application of the Special Prosecutor in the name of the United States.

(2) Whether a federal court is bound by the assertion by the President of an absolute "executive privilege" to withhold demonstrably material evidence from the trial of charges of obstruction of justice by his own White House aides and party leaders upon the grounds

that he deems production to be against the public interest.

(3) Whether a claim of executive privilege based on the generalized interest in the confidentiality of government deliberations can block the prosecution's access to evidence material to the trial of charges of criminal misconduct by high government officials who participated in those deliberations, particularly where there is a *prima facie* showing that the deliberations occurred in the course of the criminal conspiracy charged in the indictment.

(4) Whether any executive privilege that otherwise might have been applicable to discussions in the offices of the President concerning Watergate had been waived.

(5) Whether the Special Prosecutor had made an adequate showing as to the relevance and admissibility of the subpoenaed items.

The President opposed the petition of the Special Prosecutor solely on the ground that it was important for the Supreme Court to consider the case only after careful reflection and deliberation and with the aid of decisions by the lower courts. The President also stated that "it is at least questionable whether it is in the best interests of all parties involved to rush to judgment in this case in the midst of an impeachment inquiry involving intrinsically related matters."

On May 31, the Supreme Court granted the Special Prosecutor's petition and directed the parties to file their briefs simultaneously on June 21. Reply briefs would be filed on July 1, and oral argument was set for July 8.

After the Supreme Court granted the Special Prosecutor's petition, the President filed a cross-petition raising the sole question whether the grand jury has the authority to charge an incumbent President as an unindicted co-conspirator in a criminal proceeding.[14] The Supreme Court granted the cross-petition on June 15, setting the same briefing and argument schedule as for the petition of the Special Prosecutor.

The brief for the Special Prosecutor basically presented the same arguments previously outlined in the District Court and in the previous October's Court of Appeal case. The only new areas involved the questions whether the Court had jurisdiction over the dispute between the President and the Special Prosecutor and whether the grand jury had the power to name the President as an unindicted co-conspirator. The Special Prosecutor initially was undecided about addressing the question of jurisdiction in his brief because it had not been presented by the petition of either party. Since the issue of the Court's jurisdiction, however, can be raised at any time in any judicial proceeding, he determined to brief the issue fully at the outset, instead of waiting to reply to any argument by the President that the Court lacked jurisdiction.[15] As for the second issue—whether the President was subject to being named an unindicted co-conspirator—it was decided as a matter of strategy to treat the question only briefly in a long footnote to the argument that there can be no privilege when there is a showing that the subpoenaed conversations occurred in the course of a criminal conspiracy. The full development of the argument that the President is subject to being named a co-conspirator was left to the reply brief.

---

14. On June 15, the Court, on the joint motion of the Special Prosecutor and counsel for the President, unsealed the grand jury's finding.

15. This decision was influenced by the exchange of correspondence among Jaworski, St Clair and Saxbe in which Jaworski charged that the President's challenge to Jaworski's jurisdiction violated the assurances of independence that he had received when he was appointed.

The President's brief, in addition to presenting the arguments made in the District Court, claimed that the President's absolute prerogative to withhold the tapes from the courts rested in the constitutional right to privacy and freedom of expression, as well as the separation of powers. The President also argued that the Court could not ignore the pending impeachment inquiry and that enforcement of the subpoena would thrust the courts—unconstitutionally—into that controversy.

Following oral argument, the Supreme Court on July 24, affirmed Judge Sirica's order enforcing the trial subpoena.[16] First, the Court held that it had jurisdiction in the dispute between the President and the Special Prosecutor because the regulations establishing WSPF were binding on the executive branch and guaranteed the Special Prosecutor's independence from control by the Attorney General and the President. According to the Court, the dispute, stemming from the claim of privilege in the face of a judicial demand for evidence relevant and admissible in a criminal case, was the type of dispute traditionally adjudicated by the courts. The Court then held that under the Constitution the courts ultimately must determine what the constitutional powers of each branch are and the courts have the ultimate power to decide whether a claim of privilege is well taken in a judicial proceeding. The Court then rejected the claim of an absolute executive privilege, holding that although the privilege is constitutionally based (the first time this had been decided firmly by the Supreme Court) it is subject to a balance.

We conclude that when the ground for asserting privilege as to subpoenaed material sought for use in a criminal trial

---

16. The decision was unanimous with one Justice having disqualified himself.

is based only on the generalized interest in confidentiality, it cannot prevail over the fundamental demands of due process of law in the fair administration of criminal justice. The generalized assertion of privilege must yield to the demonstrated, specific need for evidence in a pending criminal trial.

Finally, the Court held that Judge Sirica had acted within his discretion in finding that the Special Prosecutor's show-ing had satisfied the burden required for the issuance of a trial subpoena.

The Court did not reach the issue raised by the President in his cross-petition—whether a President is sub-ject to being named as an unindicted co-conspirator by the grand jury. Because the Court found that the interest in confidentiality did not prevail over the need for evidence in a criminal prosecution, it was unnecessary for the Court to decide whether the privilege also was vitiated because the conversations occurred in the course of a criminal con-spiracy. Accordingly, the Court dismissed the cross-petition as "improvidently granted."

The day the Supreme Court's opinion was filed, the President announced that he would comply. The next day the Special Prosecutor filed a motion before Judge Sirica for an order implementing compliance with the Judge's earlier order of May 20, enforcing the subpoena. Less than a week later, St Clair produced the first set of subpoenaed recordings for court review.[17] Then, on August 5, before he

17. Under procedures first set forth in *Nixon* v. *Sirica* and incorporated in Judge Sirica's order of May 20, all subpoenaed recordings (with the excep-tion of those conversations that had not been recorded) were produced for inspection by the Judge. After reviewing the recordings, all relevant por-tions were released to WSPF for use in the cover-up trial. Under the Supreme Court's decision in *United States* v. *Nixon*, all portions of the sub-poenaed recordings not actually relevant to the trial remained privileged.

was required to produce them in court, the President publicly disclosed the transcripts of his conversations of June 23, 1972. These transcripts showed his early involvement in the cover-up, and belied contrary claims he had repeatedly made to the public and to the Congress. His remaining support against impeachment in the House and conviction in the Senate quickly eroded. Four days later he resigned.

Post-resignation access to the Nixon Administration materials

A few hours before the President announced his resignation, Haig conferred briefly with Jaworski to tell him of the imminent announcement and of plans to move the Nixon Administration materials to San Clemente. He assured Jaworski, however, that the materials would be kept intact and that there would be a lawyer to respond to any requests that WSPF might have. WSPF had numerous requests outstanding and there had not been full compliance with the trial subpoena.[18]

On August 13, representatives of the Special Prosecutor met with Buzhardt and St Clair about the status of the Nixon materials. Buzhardt said that the Special Prosecutor would be notified before any steps were taken to move the materials to San Clemente, but later that day the office learned through the wire services that there were immediate plans to move the materials to San Clemente. The reports indicated that a van was being loaded with the former President's personal files. White House press statements also claimed that the Special Prosecutor had approved the transfer. WSPF immediately telephoned the

---

18. Although all of the tapes called for by the subpoena had been produced, very few of the written notes and other materials pertaining to the subpoenaed conversations (materials that the subpoena required to be produced) were provided to the court.

White House to object to the removal and the statement. The statement was retracted, and Buzhardt gave an assurance that there would be no transfer without adequate advance notice to enable the Special Prosecutor to take legal action.

On August 15, four members of the Special Prosecutor's staff met with Buzhardt and Philip W. Buchen, who that day had been named counsel to President Ford. At the outset, the WSPF representatives delivered a schedule summarizing all requests then outstanding, as well as schedules delineating possible future requests for files that the Special Prosecutor believed contained evidence relevant to his continuing investigations. The staff members stated their preference not to enter into a detailed discussion of ownership of the materials, but observed that there were strong arguments that the working papers of one Administration, as long as they are relevant to pending business of the next Administration, must be made available to the next Administration. At the same time, they emphasized their interest in reaching an amicable arrangement with former President Nixon and the Ford Administration. Buzhardt expressly assured them that nothing would be moved as long as the Special Prosecutor objected. Buzhardt further stated that he would visit the former President the following week to impress upon him the urgency of securing a representative to enter into discussions with WSPF to explore possible means of providing WSPF with access to the materials it needed to complete its investigation. At the conclusion of the meeting, it was announced by joint agreement that the status of the materials in which the Special Prosecutor had a continuing interest would be maintained pending discussions.

Following the meeting, Buchen requested the Attorney General to prepare an opinion on the question of ownership of the Nixon materials. Upon receiving informal advice from the Department of Justice that the former President owned the materials, Buchen, on behalf of President Ford, without any notice to WSPF, entered into discussions with Herbert J. Miller, Jr, counsel to the former President, concerning a depository agreement regarding future custody of the Nixon tapes and documents.

On September 8, President Ford announced that he had granted a full and unconditional pardon to his predecessor for any offenses he might have committed during his tenure as President. At the same time, President Ford made public a September 7 agreement between Arthur F. Sampson, the Administrator of General Services, and former President Nixon whereby all "historical materials" of the Nixon Administration would be deposited in a secure federal facility in California. Under the terms of the agreement, once the materials were deposited, all requests or subpoenas for the materials would have to be directed to the former President who would have sole control over who could gain access to them. President Ford also announced the Attorney General's formal opinion that former President Nixon owned all the materials in question.

On September 12 members of the Special Prosecutor's staff met with Buchen and representatives of the Department of Justice. The WSPF representatives stated their belief that the Nixon-Sampson agreement violated the assurances given to the Special Prosecutor on August 15. The Special Prosecutor was willing, if necessary, to challenge the validity of the agreement. As a result, the Justice Department undertook discussions with Miller to determine whether a "modification" of the agreement could be reached to accommodate the interests of the Special Prosecutor.

Over the following days there were a series of meetings between Miller and the Department on the one hand and the Department and WSPF on the other.

The discussions included a proposal that the Special Prosecutor's requests for Nixon materials be submitted to an arbitration panel composed of a designee of the former President, a designee of the Special Prosecutor, and a third person to be chosen by the other two members of the panel. In making decisions, the arbitration panel would apply the same standards and principles that would be applicable in a court of competent jurisdiction. Negotiations over the details of a possible agreement also were carried on directly between Miller and representatives of the Special Prosecutor. They eventually broke down, however, over two principal issues—whether there would be any judicial review of the arbitration panel's decisions and whether the arbitration agreement would make any statement regarding the legislation then pending in the Congress to abrogate the Nixon-Sampson agreement. During these negotiations former President Nixon voluntarily provided materials that WSPF requested for the Watergate cover-up trial.

On October 17, former President Nixon brought suit in the United States District Court for the District of Columbia against Sampson, Buchen and H. Stuart Knight, the Director of the Secret Service (the custodian of many of the Nixon materials), to compel enforcement of the September 7 agreement or, in the alternative, to require delivery of all the tapes and documents to him in California. The Special Prosecutor intervened in this suit to protect and preserve his interests in the Presidential materials. A temporary restraining order by the court maintained the status quo and permitted access to the materials only with the joint consent of the former President and counsel for President Ford.

Thereafter, the Special Prosecutor issued grand jury subpoenas to Buchen for Nixon materials which the office believed to be relevant and important to its pending investigations. On November 9, following discussions among counsel for President Ford, the Department of Justice and the Special Prosecutor, the President determined that "the due administration of justice and the public interest require that the Special Prosecutor have prompt and effective use of those Presidential materials of the Nixon Administration now located in the White House complex that are relevant and important to ongoing criminal investigations and prosecutions within the Special Prosecutor's jurisdiction." The Special Prosecutor then entered into an agreement with Buchen, Sampson and Knight whereby WSPF would gain access to the materials to conduct a limited search for the relevant documents and tapes. The subpoenas issued to Buchen were then withdrawn.

Because of the outstanding temporary restraining order, it was necessary for the Special Prosecutor and the Department of Justice to apply to the court for a modification of the terms of the order to permit implementation of the November 9 agreement. Former President Nixon, of course, opposed the modification. The Special Prosecutor argued to the court that even if the former President were the owner of the materials, the current Administration had a right to use them in conducting important ongoing governmental business and that the former President had no right to assert executive privilege to prevent access to such use. In seeking this modification the Special Prosecutor hoped that the Court would be convinced to separate a prosecutor's interests from that of others seeking access to the materials and to meet the need for an expeditious ruling on the request.

These hopes were not realized. The Court continued to defer action on this request until it determined the entire matter relating to all claimants. The motion to amend the temporary restraining order was not granted immediately, and it appeared that there might be extended litigation before the November 9 agreement could be carried out. Accordingly, the Special Prosecutor resumed negotiations with Miller in an effort to reach a mutually acceptable agreement to afford the Special Prosecutor use of the limited number of materials that were relevant to his investigations. These negotiations lasted for approximately six weeks and included numerous meetings. Each side drafted various proposals which were debated at length. Basically, under the agreement as finally proposed, however, the Special Prosecutor would make requests similar to those he would have made under the November 9 agreement. Miller, however, would review all requested recordings as well as his client's personal files, while WSPF would review the files of White House staff members. The Special Prosecutor would have the right of access to all materials pertinent to the investigations designated in his requests that were located during these reviews. In the end, this phase of the negotiations failed to produce agreement. It became apparent that Miller, either through insertion of specific language he wanted in the agreement or merely by its timing, could use an agreement as leverage to attempt to prevent the then pending Presidential Recordings and Materials Preservation Act from becoming law. The Special Prosecutor determined that it would be inappropriate to allow his office to be placed in the posture of signing an agreement which could jeopardize the chances that the bill would become law.

The Act as signed into law on December 19 did not make it possible, however, for the Special Prosecutor to gain access to the materials he sought without extended litigation. Indeed, on December 20 former President Nixon filed an action challenging the constitutionality of the Act. WSPF and Miller then reopened negotiations, which resulted in an informal understanding that was implemented between late February and July, 1975. Under this

agreement indices of portions of the Nixon materials identified by the Special Prosecutor were prepared by
professional archivists. The Special Prosecutor, using these
various indices, designated files to be searched for materials
pertinent to investigations. He further described the investigations to allow the person examining the files to
determine which documents were in fact pertinent to the
specified investigations. With a limited number of excep-
tions—those files that contained highly personal or
confidential communications of former President Nixon—
the file searches were conducted by archivists assigned to
White House counsel's office. All documents located in any
file reviewed that were relevant to any of the specified
investigations were supplied to WSPF. It was agreed, however, that notes of Haldeman and Ehrlichman meetings
with the President would be turned over if they pertained
to the specific investigation designated for the file in which
they were found. Furthermore, all requested recordings
were reviewed by Miller or an associate, and if there were
any conversations on the recordings with information
pertinent to the Special Prosecutor's investigations, copies
of those conversations were made available. WSPF was also
permitted to listen to any recording if there was any
question as to its pertinence. This procedure provided
WSPF with much information needed for pending trials
and for conclusion of several investigations.

The final dealings with former President Nixon
involved WSPF's taking of his testimony under oath, in the
presence of two grand jurors, in California on June 23 and
24, 1975. A stipulation filed with the court stated that the
grand jury believed it was necessary to obtain the testimony of the former President concerning several areas of
ongoing inquiry. Upon his representation that he was willing to submit to questioning, but unwilling to travel to
Washington because of his doctor's advice, and in view of

other legal considerations, the grand jury consented to a sworn examination in California. This procedure was approved by the court and the transcript was later presented to the full grand jury and made part of its minutes.

ACTIONS RELATED TO PRESIDENT NIXON'S POSSIBLE CRIMINAL LIABILITY

Background
Speculation about the President's possible involvement in Watergate-related offenses, stemming largely from press reports, predated the appointment of the Special Prosecutor. Later, during televised hearings before the Senate Select Committee, Senator Howard Baker repeatedly expressed this concern by asking "What did the President know and when did he know it?" Responsibility for any criminal investigation of this question was given to the Special Prosecutor. His charter gave "full authority for investigating and prosecuting . . . allegations involving the President."

Direct evidence linking President Nixon to the Watergate cover-up came from former White House counsel John Dean, when he testified publicly before the Senate Select Committee in June 1973. Dean told the Committee that President Nixon had discussed executive clemency for Watergate burglar Howard Hunt with his former aide Charles Colson, and that the President had approved the payment of money to Hunt in return for his silence. Dean's account of two crucial meetings with Nixon and of the President's approval of raising further "hush money" was contradicted by former White House aide H. R. Haldeman, who testified before the Committee that the President had told Dean with respect to the money: "We could do that, but it would be wrong." In the summer of 1973, at Cox's request, WSPF staff prepared the same kind of factual memorandum about any possible criminal involvement of the President as had been prepared with respect to other major actors. At this stage, the Watergate task force memorandum relied heavily on Dean's uncorroborated testimony.

After the "Saturday Night Massacre" of October 20, 1973, WSPF received seven subpoenaed tape recordings of Presidential conversations which had taken place from September 15, 1972, to April 16, 1973. Of particular significance was the tape of the March 21, 1973, morning meeting among the President, Haldeman, and Dean, which recorded the following discussion about payment to the Watergate burglars:

> *President:* How much money do you need?
>
> *Dean:* I would say these people are going to cost, ah, a million dollars over the next, ah, few years.
>
> *President:* We could get that.
>
> *Dean:* Um huh.
>
> *President:* You, on, the money, you need the money. I mean, ah, you can get the money, but its . . .
>
> *Dean:* Well I think that we're . . .
>
> *President:* My point is, you can, you can get a million dollars, and you can get it in cash. Ah, I know where it could be got.
>
> *Dean:* Um huh.
>
> *President:* I mean, ah, it's not easy, but it could be done. But, ah, the question is, who the hell would handle it?
>
> *Dean:* That is right. Ah.
>
> *President:* Any ideas on that?
>
> *Dean:* Well I would think that would be something Mitchell ought to be charged with.
>
> *President:* I would think so too.

* * * * *

President: That's right, that's why, that's why your immediate thing, you've got no choice with Hunt with a hundred and twenty or whatever it is. Right?

Dean: That's right.

President: Would you agree that that's the buy time thing and you better damn well get that done.

Dean: I think that he ought to be given some signal anyway to, to . . .

President: . . . Well for Christ's sake get it, in a way that, ah—who, who's gonna talk to him? Colson? He's the one who is supposed to know him.

This tape recording and others received by the Special Prosecutor in December substantially corroborated and added significantly to Dean's allegations. In January 1974, and as argued later at the cover-up trial, the Watergate task force concluded that President Nixon had known prior to March 21, 1973, about the existence of a conspiracy to obstruct justice on the part of his closest White House aides and high officials of his Re-Election Committee, and that on March 21, when the President learned many of the material details of the cover-up and the potential criminal liability of those involved, he had furthered the conspiracy by urging that a cash payment be made to Howard Hunt to "buy time" and by discussing a possible strategy of continuing the cover-up by limited disclosure of some information together with continued concealment of the most damaging evidence. On receiving this analysis, Special Prosecutor Jaworski sought to determine whether an incumbent President could be indicted for a crime.

Determining whether to seek the President's indictment

Counsel to the Special Prosecutor and his staff conducted extensive legal research to resolve whether the

Constitution contemplated the impeachment process as the exclusive means for adjudicating the culpability of an incumbent President. As they found, that issue had been largely ignored or only obliquely alluded to at the time of the Constitutional Convention and in the ensuing 186 years.

The question of the President's indictability, which was viewed in the office as obviously momentous in terms of its consequences for the country, resulted in an intense debate among members of the Special Prosecutor's staff. After examining the Constitution, relevant case law, and the historical and contemporary arguments, there appeared to be no textual basis in the Constitution for concluding that an incumbent President—any more than any other Federal official subject to the impeachment process—is immune from the ordinary process of criminal law prior to impeachment and removal from office. Consequently, one approach was that, if a *prima facie* case of obstruction of justice existed on the basis of known evidence, an indict-ment of the President would be essential to vindicate the principles that there should be equal justice for all and that no one is above the law. This view held that a failure to indict the incumbent President, in the face of evidence of his criminal activity, would seriously impair the integrity of the criminal process. Such impairment would be all the more severe because the President was the very man in whom the Constitution reposes the final obligation to ensure that the law is obeyed and enforced, and because his actions appeared to have been designed to place himself and other individuals beyond the reach of the law.

The other approach was that the impeachment process should take precedence over a criminal indictment because the Constitution was ambivalent on this point and an indictment provoking a necessarily lengthy legal proceed-ing would either compel the President's resignation or substantially cripple his ability to function effectively in the domestic and foreign fields as the Nation's Chief Executive Officer. Those consequences, it was argued, should result from the impeachment mechanism explicitly provided by the Constitution, a mechanism in which the elected representatives of the public conduct preliminary inquiries and, in the event of the filing of a bill of impeachment of the President, a trial based upon all the facts. Any indictment could then be brought after those proceedings were completed. Under this view, a single, unelected prosecutor should be hesitant to invoke the criminal justice system, prior to the completion of pending impeachment hearings, especially when the constitutionality of such a course remained in doubt. There was also concern that an indictment of the President would suspend the impeachment proceedings until after his criminal trial.

The Special Prosecutor concluded that the Supreme Court, if presented with the question, would not uphold an indictment of the President for the crimes of which he would be accused. Accordingly, he thought it would not be responsible conduct to recommend that the grand jury return an indictment against the President, particularly when the impeachment proceedings were ongoing. Since the Special Prosecutor's charter mandated his investigating allegations against the President and authorized reports to the Congress, he then examined the legality of a grand jury presentment concerning President Nixon, and the possible transmission of evidence pertinent to the question of his involvement to the House of Representatives. After additional legal research and deliberation within the office, the Special Prosecutor determined that this course of action would be both constitutional and appropriate. It was his view that the House of Representatives, in the first instance, was the appropriate body under the Constitution to examine evidence relating to the President, and to determine whether he should be charged with conduct justifying impeachment and removal from office. Many alternatives for the form of such a report were considered; the possibilities included a presentment detailing all the evidence in narrative form, a conclusory summary of grand jury findings of fact and conclusions of law, or a transmission of relevant witness testimony without comment or conclusions. The Special Prosecutor advised the grand jury to submit a report with evidence relating to the President to Judge Sirica, and to recommend that the Judge transmit such evidence to the House Judiciary Committee.

In order to avoid any claim of unilateral action on the part of the Special Prosecutor in the event that he should name the President as a co-conspirator during pretrial pro-ceedings in the Watergate case, Jaworski also sought the grand jury's judgment on his opinion that the President was a member of the charged conspiracy and that evidentiary considerations at a cover-up trial mandated naming the President as a participant in the conspiracy. Thus, when the grand jury voted to indict seven men in connection with the Watergate cover-up, it also voted to name Richard M. Nixon as one of the 18 unindicted co-conspirators in an alleged conspiracy to obstruct justice.

At the time the grand jury handed up the indictment on March 1, it also submitted a Report and Recommen-dation advising the Chief Judge that it "had heard evidence that it regards as having a material bearing on matters within the primary jurisdiction" of the House Judiciary Committee in its impeachment inquiry, but that it ought "to defer to the House of Representatives" in determining what action was warranted by the evidence. The grand jury recommended that the sealed materials accompanying the report be transmitted to the House Judiciary Committee. The materials included 12 recordings of Presidential con-versations and testimony pertinent to President Nixon's involvement in the Watergate matter.

In a March 6 hearing before Judge Sirica on the disposition of the grand jury report, James St Clair announced for the President that he would furnish to the Judiciary Committee all the materials that had previously been furnished to the Special Prosecutor's office. The Special Prosecutor's counsel argued that the materials the White House had agreed to supply to the Committee were not necessarily the same as those the grand jury asked the court to transmit to the Committee. John Doar and Albert Jenner, appearing on behalf of the Committee, requested that the Court deliver the grand jury report to enable the Committee to discharge its constitutional obligation with the aid of the best information available. In a March 8 letter from Committee Chairman Peter Rodino to Judge Sirica, Rodino stated that a unanimous resolution of the Committee reflected its view that in constitutional terms it would be unthinkable if the material was kept from the House of Representatives. Judge Sirica ruled on March 18 that the grand jury report and accompanying materials should be delivered to the Committee.

On March 20, two defendants named in the Watergate cover-up indictment, H. R. Haldeman and Gordon Strachan, filed a petition for a writ of mandamus with the Court of Appeals to block the delivery of the materials to the Committee. The next day, the Court denied the petition, stating that the President, as the focus of the grand jury report and the person who presumably would have the greatest interest in its disposition, interposed no objection to the District Court's action. As a result, the report was delivered to the House Judiciary Committee on March 26. In addition, the President delivered to the Committee the materials he had given to the Special Prosecutor. These included 12 recordings related to Watergate, seven related to ITT, dairy, and "Plumbers" matters, and numerous documents relevant to these areas.

Cooperation with the House Judiciary Committee

House Resolution 803, adopted by the House of Representatives on February 6, by a vote of 410 to 4, explicitly authorized the House Judiciary Committee to investigate whether grounds existed for the impeachment of Richard Nixon. The resolution also granted the Committee the power of subpoena for its investigation. Preliminary discussions on liaison between the staff of the House Judiciary Committee and the Special Prosecutor's office had been held more than two months earlier. In a meeting on November 20, 1973, between attorneys from the Special Prosecutor's office and the Judiciary Committee, Deputy Special Prosecutor Ruth had assured the Committee of WSPF's cooperation so long as such cooperation did not interfere with WSPF investigations and trials and investigative sources were protected.

Ruth's pledge was subsequently honored by WSPF, despite a minor problem which arose in February 1974, when the Committee requested a detailed list of recordings, documents and other material the Special Prosecutor had received from the White House, plus a list of the requests for evidence that had not been met. Special Prosecutor Jaworski's original position was that Rule 6(e) of the Federal Rules of Criminal Procedure, which bars disclosure of matters occurring before a grand jury, prevented him from revealing this information. However, when St Clair stated he had no objection, Jaworski supplied the Committee with the requested lists. On February 25, after the Judiciary Committee received the list of materials obtained by the Special Prosecutor from the White House, Doar asked the White House to furnish the Committee with copies of certain materials, including 19 tape recordings of Presidential conversations theretofore given to the Special Prosecutor, and all tape recordings, notes and other writings relating to 42 specifically identified Presidential conversations which had been supplied to the Special Prosecutor.[19]

As the Judiciary Committee's inquiry progressed, its attorneys recognized the need to gain access to materials under seal of the court in a number of "Watergate"-related cases. In each instance, the Committee directed a formal motion to the court, with a request to the Special Prosecutor to state his position. Responding to such an application in April by the Committee,[20] Jaworski stated that he had no objection to having Committee staff review the material but was opposed to unsealing it. In one instance, Jaworski opposed access to the record of the medical examination of ITT lobbyist Dita Beard on the grounds that the results of the examination were not relevant to the Committee's inquiry and that disclosure would be unwarranted intrusion on Beard's rights. Jaworski also objected to access to grand jury testimony submitted to Judge Gesell in the prosecution of former White House aide Dwight

---

19. The 42 Presidential conversations were not provided, and on April 11, 1974, the House Judiciary Committee issued the first of eight subpoenas directed to the President. In partial response to the subpoena, the President on April 30, supplied to the Committee, and released publicly, edited transcripts of 31 of the 42 subpoenaed conversations, claiming that the other 11 conversations had either not been recorded or could not be located. On May 1, the Judiciary Committee formally advised the President by letter that he had failed to comply with its subpoena. The President's failure to comply with this and other subpoenas formed the basis for Article III of Impeachment later adopted by the House Judiciary Committee.

20. The application sought material under seal in connection with the following matters: *United States* v. *Chapin*, Crim. No. 990–73; *United States* v. *Krogh*, Crim. No. 857–73; *In Re Grand Jury Proceedings*, Misc. 47–73; *In Re Grand Jury Proceedings*, Misc. 108–73; *United States* v. *Liddy, et al.*, Crim. No. 1827–72; *Halperin* v. *Kissinger, et al.*, Civil No. 1187–73; *Ellsberg, et al.* v. *Mitchell, et al.*, Civil No. 1879–72; *Nader* v. *Internal Revenue Service*, Civil No. 1851–72; *Nader* v. *Butz*, Civil No. 148–72; *Common Cause* v. *Finance Committee to Re-Elect the President, et al.*, Civil No. 1780–72.

Chapin, due to the provisions of Rule 6(e). In May, the Judiciary Committee again requested access to additional materials sealed by the court,[21] and again Jaworski was asked to state his position. The Special Prosecutor replied that he had no objection to the granting of the Committee's access to these materials, since they did not appear likely to prejudice any individuals. In addition to sealed materials, the Judiciary Committee also requested copies of the grand jury testimony of Egil Krogh, David Young and Henry Petersen in connection with the indictment returned in the Fielding break-in case. This testimony was supplied to the Committee by the court.

The Special Prosecutor's office also supplied information directly to the Committee throughout the impeachment inquiry. The basis for WSPF's action was set forth in a May 8 letter from Jaworski to Doar in which the Special Prosecutor stated his understanding that, although WSPF was being asked to provide the information voluntarily, the Committee was prepared to fulfill its responsibilities by issuing subpoenas. On the basis of this understanding, Jaworski determined that his office would furnish such relevant information requested by the Committee as it possessed, within the bounds of relevant laws and regulations. Jaworski also informed Doar that WSPF staff attorneys would contact Committee staff attorneys to coordinate the furnishing of requested information.

---

21. These were the May 13, 1974, transcripts of *in camera* hearings on the President's motion to quash the April 18 subpoena issued in *United States* v. *Mitchell, et al.*, the May 13, 1974, transcripts of *in camera* hearings on the tape experts' report and a pre-publication copy of the report. In addition, the Judiciary Committee requested permission to listen to the June 20, June 30, and September 15, 1972, conversations to determine whether they were relevant to the Committee's inquiry.

On May 9, Ruth notified WSPF task force leaders of the procedures to be followed in providing information to the Committee: there could be no disclosure of testimony presented before a grand jury; no disclosure of information received from the White House (Doar was arranging to receive from St Clair what the White House had supplied to the Special Prosecutor); documentary evidence would be furnished only when the source of the information consented (the same procedure used with the Senate Select Committee); only information directly related to possible Presidential involvement would be furnished; confidentiality of witnesses would be preserved if necessary; and no notes of office interviews were to be supplied. Ruth further directed that WSPF staff members recommend the names of witnesses to be interviewed by the Committee and the topics to be covered in such interviews.

Pursuant to this arrangement, the Special Prosecutor's office provided the impeachment inquiry staff with numerous investigative leads and with non-grand jury materials. Doar was permitted to examine, in the Special Prosecutor's office, a summary memorandum concerning "allegations involving the President." In addition, the Committee reviewed WSPF's copies of White House transcripts of Nixon-Dean conversations between September 15, 1972, and April 16, 1973, to determine if there were any discrepancies between them and the transcripts published in the President's submission to the Committee. The prosecutors also attempted to save the Committee's time by steering its investigation away from allegations that WSPF had already determined to be frivolous or unfounded.

Since one of its areas of investigation was the relationship between the White House and WSPF and the extent of White House cooperation with the Special Prosecutor, the Committee requested and received from the Special Prosecutor's office copies of correspondence and memoranda relating to material sought from the White House by Special Prosecutors Cox and Jaworski. WSPF also supplied to the Committee materials on Cox's relations with the White House and with Attorney General Richardson and on Jaworski's relations with the White House.

Cooperation between WSPF and the Committee was mutual. The Special Prosecutor requested information from the Committee to provide defendants with prior statements and testimony of Government witnesses relating to their trial testimony as well as any material in the Government's possession favorable to the defendants. Although WSPF contended that transmission of Congressional testimony to defendants was not required by law, the office voluntarily provided such information, including Committee staff interviews of Egil Krogh for the Fielding break-in trial, staff interviews and statements of individuals connected with the Watergate cover-up trial, and staff interviews and documents of individuals having knowledge of President Nixon's tax returns and personal finances.

As a result of the Committee's investigation, on June 18 and 19, 1974, Doar presented to the Committee a "Statement of Information" containing evidence on the events that led to the appointment of Elliot Richardson as Attorney General, the creation of the Watergate Special Prosecution Force, the appointment of Archibald Cox, the authority and jurisdiction of the Special Prosecutor's office, the investigations initiated by the Special Prosecutor and the response of President Nixon to those investigations, the issuance of subpoenas to the President, the litigation arising out of his refusal to comply with those subpoenas, the firing of Cox, the appointment of Leon Jaworski, and the court hearings on the 18½-minute erasure on the June 20, 1972, tape.

On July 29, by a vote of 28 to 10, the Committee adopted a second Article of Impeachment against President Nixon. Article II charged that the President had:

> ... repeatedly engaged in conduct violating the constitutional rights of citizens, impairing the due and proper administration of justice and the conduct of lawful inquiries, or contravening the laws governing agencies of the executive branch and the purposes of these agencies.

As an example of such conduct, the Committee stated:

> In disregard of the rule of law, he knowingly misused the executive power by interfering with agencies of the executive branch, including the Federal Bureau of Investigation, the Criminal Division and the Office of Watergate Special Prosecution Force, of the Department of Justice, and the Central Intelligence Agency, in violation of his duty to take care that the laws be faithfully executed.

As supporting evidence for its conclusion that President Nixon had impeded the Special Prosecutor's investigation, the Committee noted the White House delay in making information available to the Special Prosecutor and, in some cases, withholding documents, the concealment of the White House taping system, the firing of Cox, and the refusal to cooperate with Jaworski.

The President's resignation; further consideration of indictment

On July 24, 1974, the Supreme Court announced its unanimous decision in *United States* v. *Nixon* and ordered the President to turn over additional tape recordings of Presidential conversations subpoenaed for use in the Watergate cover-up trial then scheduled to begin in

September. Among the subpoenaed conversations were those of June 23, 1972, between H. R. Haldeman and the President. On Monday, August 5, St Clair and Alexander Haig, the President's chief of staff, telephoned Jaworski to inform him that the June 23 tape recording revealed the President's early knowledge of the Watergate cover-up and a possible violation of law in his misuse of a Federal agency. On Thursday, August 8, Jaworski met with Haig at the latter's request. Jaworski later told members of his staff that Haig had called the meeting to inform him of the President's decision to resign, but that during the meeting no promises or understandings of any kind had been either requested or offered. In a statement issued immediately after the President's resignation announcement, the Special Prosecutor said:

> There has been no agreement or understanding of any sort between the President or his representatives and the Special Prosecutor relating in any way to the President's resignation.
>
> The Special Prosecutor's Office was not asked for any such agreement or understanding and offered none. Although I was informed of the President's decision this afternoon, my office did not participate in any way in the President's decision to resign.

President Nixon's resignation became effective at noon on Friday, August 9. Shortly thereafter Jaworski was contacted by Herbert J. Miller, Jr, an attorney for the former President. During several meetings between Jaworski and Miller in August, Miller argued that the former President should not be indicted because the massive publicity resulting from both the impeachment proceedings and his resignation would make it impossible to select an impartial jury. On September 4, Miller submitted to the Special Prosecutor an extensive memorandum supporting this view. Research by the WSPF staff disputed Miller's position, however, and Jaworski concluded that any prosecution of the former President might require a nine-month to one-year delay in bringing a case to trial in order to allow existing and foreseeable pretrial publicity to dissipate.

Another question raised in the wake of the resignation was whether the former President should be included as a defendant in the Watergate cover-up case. Jaworski invited members of WSPF's legal staff to submit their views on this question and other issues surrounding possible criminal action against the former President, and many did. Since it was evident to the Special Prosecutor and to staff members that inclusion of the former President would entail considerable if not indefinite delay of the trial, which was then scheduled to begin on October 1, Jaworski decided against such inclusion. He also decided to defer any criminal action against the former President until the cover-up jury was sequestered, to eliminate the possibility that the jurors might be subjected to additional pretrial publicity.

The pardon

On August 28, President Ford held a nationally televised press conference, his first since taking office. During that press conference, the President answered several questions regarding a possible pardon for his predecessor:

Q: Mr President, aside from the Special Prosecutor's role, do you agree with the Bar Association that the laws apply equally to all men, or do you agree with Governor Rockefeller that former President Nixon should have immunity from prosecution, and specifically, would you use your pardon authority, if necessary?

A : Well, let me say at the outset that I made a statement in this
room in the few months [sic] after the swearing-in, and on
that occasion I said the following: That I had hoped that
our former President, who brought peace to millions,
would find it for himself.

Now, the expression made by Governor Rockefeller, I
think, coincides with the general view and the point of
view of the American people. I subscribe to that point of
view, but let me add in the last ten days or two weeks I
have asked for prayers for guidance on this very important
point.

In this situation, I am the final authority. There have
been no charges made, there has been no action by
the courts, there has been no action by any jury,
and until any legal process has been undertaken,
I think it is unwise and untimely for me to make any
commitment.

★　★　★　★　★

Q: May I just follow up on Helen's question: You are saying,
sir, that the option of a pardon for former President Nixon
is still an option that you will consider, depending on what
the courts will do.

A : Of course, I make the final decision. Until it gets to me, I
make no commitment one way or the other. But I do have
the right as President of the United States to make that
decision.

Q: And you are not ruling it out?

A : I am not ruling it out. It is an option and a proper option
for any President.

Q: Do you feel the Special Prosecutor can in good conscience
pursue cases against former top Nixon aides as long as there
is the possibility that the former President may not also be
pursued in the courts?

A : I think the Special Prosecutor, Mr Jaworski, has an obligation to take whatever action he sees fit in conformity with
his oath of office, and that should include any and all
individuals.

★ ★ ★ ★ ★

Q: Mr President, you have emphasized here your option of
granting a pardon to the former President.

A : I intend to.

Q: You intend to have that option. If an indictment is brought,
would you grant a pardon before any trial took place?

A : I said at the outset that until the matter reaches me, I am
not going to make any comment during the process of
whatever charges are made.

Jaworski had made it plain to staff members that he would
not seek the former President's indictment if President
Ford intended to pardon him. Accordingly, he met with
Philip W. Buchen, President Ford's counsel, on September
4. Jaworski reported later to staff members that during this
meeting he had advised Buchen that the President's statements at the press conference had put the Special
Prosecutor in a "peculiar position" since the President's
comments suggested that any action taken by WSPF against
former President Nixon might prove to be futile. Jaworski
also reported that he had made no recommendation to
Buchen concerning a possible pardon, since he considered
the issue to be wholly the President's prerogative and felt
that it would be inappropriate for him to make an un-
solicited recommendation. At Buchen's request as to the
probable length of time between an indictment and a trial,
Jaworski delivered to him a letter expressing the following
view on trial delay:

The factual situation regarding a trial of Richard M. Nixon within constitutional bounds, is unprecedented. It is especially unique in view of the recent House Judiciary Committee inquiry on impeachment, resulting in a unanimous adverse finding to Richard M. Nixon on the Article involving obstruction of justice. The massive publicity given the hearings and the findings that ensued, the reversal of judgment of a number of the members of the Republican Party following release of the June 23 tape recording, and their statements carried nationwide, and finally, the resignation of Richard M. Nixon, require a delay, before selection of a jury is begun, of a period from nine months to a year, and perhaps even longer. This judgment is predicated on a review of the decisions of United States Courts involving prejudicial pretrial publicity. The Government's decision to pursue impeachment proceedings and the tremendous volume of television, radio and newspaper coverage given thereto, are factors emphasized by the Courts in weighing the time a trial can be had. The complexities involved in the process of selecting a jury and the time it will take to complete the process, I find difficult to estimate at this time.

The situation involving Richard M. Nixon is readily distinguishable from the facts involved in the case of *United States* v. *Mitchell, et al.* [the Watergate cover-up case] set for trial on September 30th. The defendants in the Mitchell case were indicted by a grand jury operating in secret session. They will be called to trial, unlike Richard M. Nixon, if indicted, without any previous adverse finding by an investigatory body holding public hearings on its conclusions. It is precisely the condemnation of Richard M. Nixon already made in the impeachment process, that would make it unfair to the defendants in the case of *United States* v. *Mitchell, et al.*, for Richard M. Nixon now to be joined as a co-conspirator, should it be concluded that an indictment of him was proper.

The *United States* v. *Mitchell, et al.,* trial will within itself generate new publicity, some undoubtedly prejudicial to Richard M. Nixon. I bear this in mind when I estimate the earliest time of trial of Richard M. Nixon under his constitutional guarantees, in the event of indictment, to be as indicated above.

During their meeting, Jaworski also submitted to Buchen a memorandum prepared by Deputy Special Prosecutor Ruth, listing ten matters under investigation which "may prove to have some direct connection to activities in which Mr Nixon is personally involved." The memorandum cautioned that "none of these matters at the moment rises to the level of our ability to prove even a probable criminal violation by Mr Nixon." The memorandum explicitly stated, however, that it was not intended to deal with the former President's possible liability in connection with the Watergate cover-up.

On September 8, President Ford granted a "full, free and absolute" pardon to former President Nixon for all offenses committed during Mr Nixon's tenure as President (January 20, 1969, through August 9, 1974). President Ford's action generated extensive discussion and legal research by WSPF.

This focused upon two possible theories to challenge the pardon. First, was it invalid because it preceded any indictment or conviction? And second, despite the President's inherent constitutional powers to control all law enforcement decisions, whether by directing that an investigation not proceed, ordering an indictment dismissed, or granting a pardon, had the President voluntarily bound himself through the Special Prosecutor's charter not to exercise his constitutional pardon powers when the exercise of that power would interfere with the independent judgment of the Special Prosecutor to decide whom to prosecute?

The Special Prosecutor initially declined to make public any of his views concerning the pardon in view of the approaching Watergate trial and the order of the court regarding pretrial publicity. Later, after the Watergate trial jury had been sequestered, he stated the basis of his decision not to challenge the validity of the pardon in a letter to Attorney General William Saxbe, dated October 12, which accompanied his letter of resignation as Special Prosecutor:

> Although not appropriate for comment until after the sequestering of the jury in *United States* v. *Mitchell, et al.,* in view of suggestions that an indictment be returned against former President Richard M. Nixon questioning the validity of the pardon granted him, I think it proper that I express to you my views on this subject to dispel any thought that there may be some relation between my resignation and that issue.
>
> As you realize, one of my responsibilities, not only as an officer of the court, but as a prosecutor, as well, is not to take a position in which I lack faith or which my judgment dictates is not supported by probable cause. The provision in the Constitution investing the President with the right to grant pardons, and the recognition by the United States Supreme Court that a pardon may be granted prior to the filing of charges are so clear, in my opinion, as not to admit of doubt. Philip Lacovara, then Counsel to the Special Prosecutor, by written memorandum on file in this office, came to the same conclusion, pointing out that:
>
> ". . . the pardon power can be exercised at any time after a federal crime has been committed and it is not necessary that there be any criminal proceedings pending. In fact, the pardon power has been used frequently to relieve federal offenders of criminal liability and other penalties and disabilities attaching to their offenses even where no

criminal proceedings against the individual are
contemplated."

I have also concluded, after thorough study, that there is
nothing in the charter and guidelines appertaining to the
office of the Special Prosecutor that impairs or curtails the
President's free exercise of the constitutional right of
pardon.

I was co-architect, along with Acting Attorney General
Robert Bork, of the provisions some theorists now point to
as inhibiting the constitutional pardoning power of the
President. The additional safeguards of independence on
which I insisted and which Mr Bork, on former President
Nixon's authority, was willing to grant were solely for
purposes of limiting the grounds on which my discharge
could be based and not for the purpose of enlarging on the
jurisdiction of the Special Prosecutor.

Hearings held by the Senate Judiciary Committee
subsequent to my appointment make it clear that my
jurisdiction as Special Prosecutor was to be no different
from that possessed by my predecessor.

There was considerable concern expressed by some
Senators that Acting Attorney General Bork, by
supplemental order, inadvertently had limited the
jurisdiction that previously existed. The hearings fully
developed the concept that the thrust of the new provisions
giving me the aid of the Congressional "consensus"
committee were to insulate me from groundless efforts to
terminate my employment or to limit the jurisdiction that
existed. It was made clear, however, that there was no
"redefining" of the jurisdiction of the Special Prosecutor as
it existed from the beginning. There emerged from these
hearings the definite understanding that in no sense were
the additional provisions inserted in the Special Prosecutor's
Charter for the purpose of either enlarging or diminishing
his jurisdiction. I did stress, as I argued in the Supreme

Court in *US* v. *Nixon*, that I was given the verbal assurance that I could bring suit against the President to enforce subpoena rights, a point upheld by the Court. This, of course, has no bearing on the pardoning power.

I cannot escape the conclusion, therefore, that additional provisions to the Charter do not subordinate the constitutional pardoning power to the Special Prosecutor's jurisdictional rights. For me now to contend otherwise would not only be contrary to the interpretation agreed upon in Congressional hearings—it also would be, on my part, intellectually dishonest.

Thus, in light of these conclusions, for me to procure an indictment of Richard M. Nixon for the sole purpose of generating a purported court test on the legality of the pardon, would constitute a spurious proceeding in which I had no faith; in fact, it would be tantamount to unprofessional conduct and violative of my responsibility as prosecutor and officer of the court.

CONCLUDING OBSERVATIONS

Normally when prosecutors are asked to recommend reforms [not included here], the questions are limited to the criminal justice system. But most of what WSPF personnel experienced in criminal justice was dramatically atypical of criminal justice generally. The prosecutors had adequate resources; defendants were not jailed for long periods of time prior to trial; the courts had time and resources to meet all the demands of Watergate litigation in a detached, unhurried atmosphere; private defense counsel brought all their skills to thorough pretrial investigation, legal attack, trial strategy and fully briefed appeals; the sections of Federal prisons in which convicted Watergate defendants served their terms all lacked the small, inhuman spaces in which most American criminals reside, locked into their idleness for 17 hours each day; and constant press and public scrutiny provided a careful watchdog to make sure that Government investigations proceeded without abuse of power or undue leniency. Watergate did not educate American citizens about the normal, day-to-day criminal justice process.

In considering what recommendations to include in this report, WSPF concentrated on what it did observe: criminal abuse of power by Government officials in high places; historical growth of secrecy in the Federal executive branch unchecked by Americans and their elected Congress; unchallenged, subjective judgments by the executive branch in identifying persons and organizations that constitute an impermissible threat to the national interest and to executive policy; an undemocratic condition wherein money is power, and skillful, cynical public relations cements that power; and finally, a silent, sometimes grudging, sometimes willful conclusion by some Government representatives that ethical standards are irrelevant because quick implementation of policy goals is mandatory, but achievable only by social and personal injustices to others.

These conclusions all arose from observing how Government officials and agencies actually grapple with the legitimate demands upon them. The demands of national security require extraordinary judgment. The separation of powers concept requires judicious use of the privilege doctrine. Politicians cannot be elected without extensive campaign funds and loyal friends who want rewards. Individual requirements for personal success seem always to demand that one must "ride with the system." And a leader hoping to implement his policies is loathe to choose anyone whose independence or unpredictable mind may eventually undermine or delay those goals.

These demands have always had, and will continue to have, inherent potential for abuse of power. National security can easily be used to justify unconstitutional actions, and executive privilege can then be invoked to justify the failure to disclose these actions. Subjective distrust can be identified mistakenly with a national need that justified massive intelligence systems with permanent storage and illicit use of personal information. Political survival, rationalized by one's perceived ability to accomplish the national will, can too easily justify the acceptance of "big money" and the granting of instant access to any friend of one's cause or one's administration. The leader who sets out to accomplish his goals may appoint as executives only those who helped him along the political path and who will give him support that disregards independent analysis or the demands of personal will and courage.

This brief and, by no means, original or exclusive catalog should sound familiar to all readers of this report. Many of the Watergate phenomena had their historical precedents. Many had grown with no deterrence from other branches of Government. Others had grown without questions from the people and from the press. Watergate should not be analyzed merely in the context of each individual abuse of power that prosecutors were told to investigate. As with any coalescing of activities that lead to a national crisis, so too did Watergate grow from historical roots that presaged abuses of institutional power.

If Watergate was an insidious climax to recent and hitherto subtle historical trends, the formulation of recommendations must begin with the simple, but basic, observation that democracies do not survive unless elected officials do what they are supposed to do and citizens maintain vigilance to see that they do. The public unfolding of Watergate abuses resulted from citizens, press and official actions. Nothing can replace that kind of vigilance;

and recommendations for new laws or new institutions are insignificant when compared to the stubborn, plodding, daily work of Americans and their elected representatives in watching over and channeling the power of their national Government, the power of concentrated wealth, the power of officially spoken and written words, and the power of secret bureaucracies.

As prosecutors searching only for facts that disclose or disclaim criminal activity, WSPF lacks the expertise to propose a broad base of political and social change. The recommendations we make are not so intended. The proposals are modest but their implementation would probably help. Most appear easy and obvious. But that is a good way to start testing a Nation's willingness to learn from its past.

One final note, albeit a personal one. One hundred years ago, an America still recovering from its devastating Civil War wrestled with the pay-off scandals of the Grant Administration and approached its centennial celebration. Historians report that few candidates reached the United States Senate without financial support from the "special interests"—railroads, oil companies, textile concerns, the iron and steel industry and mining companies.[1] The Nation had grown so weary that even the usually optimistic Longfellow wrote:

> Ah, woe is me
> I hoped to see my country rise to heights
> Of happiness and freedom yet unreached

---

1. The historical observations are taken from Samuel Eliot Morison, *The Oxford History of the American People*. 731–3 (Oxford University Press 1965).

By other nations, but the climbing wave
Pauses, lets go its hold, and slides again
Back to the common level, with a hoarse
Death-rattle in its throat. I am too old
To hope for better days.

Now again, at the Bicentennial, the Nation has grown weary. Much contributed to this, but few can deny that uncovering years of actual and alleged Government abuses has played its part. Institutions once again had to earn the faith of the people in whose names they acted.

That lesson became clear. When Archibald Cox was fired, Americans rose in anger. The telegrams came to us from Middle America—small cities, towns, and hamlets that only the residents had ever heard of. The national Government had offended its people's sense of justice. The citizens wanted to control what would happen, and they eventually did. When vigilance erupted, institutions responded. One must believe that unresponsive power, both public and private, can never overcome that will.

APPENDIX: ORGANIZATIONAL HISTORY

This appendix is a narrative of events leading up to the formation of the Special Prosecutor's office in the spring of 1973, the organization of the office, and its eventual abolition and re-establishment, all within a five-month period.

BACKGROUND TO THE APPOINTMENT OF THE SPECIAL PROSECUTOR

By the spring of 1973 there were strong indications that "Watergate" involved more than the "third-rate burglary" described by a White House spokesman. The press had linked high officials of the Committee to Re-Elect the President with the break-in and had uncovered facts which suggested that the White House and other Federal agencies had engaged in such activities as political espionage, break-ins, obstruction of justice and irregularities in campaign financing. In short, a trail of misdeeds seemed to lead directly to the White House.

Although the President and the then Attorney General insisted that the original Watergate investigation had been exhaustive, a number of circumstances caused increasing suspicion that much more probing was necessary:

- In late February and early March, Acting FBI Director L. Patrick Gray revealed that the Bureau had investigated little other than the break-in itself and had not pursued other allegations.
- In March, one of the defendants, James McCord, wrote a letter to Judge Sirica alleging a "cover-up" of incidents surrounding the break-in. He charged that persons yet unnamed were involved in the case, that perjury had been committed at the trial of the burglars, and that political pressure had been applied to the defendants to induce them to plead guilty and remain silent.
- On April 15, Attorney General Richard Kleindienst disqualified himself from the investigation because of his close personal and professional relationship with persons under suspicion.
- On April 30, White House Press Secretary Ronald Ziegler announced the resignations of Haldeman and Ehrlichman, and the firing of Dean. In the same announcement, he revealed that Kleindienst had resigned and had been replaced by the Secretary of Defense, Elliot Richardson.

That evening in a television address to the Nation, President Nixon said that he had given Richardson absolute authority over the Watergate case and related matters, including the authority to name a Special Prosecutor if he considered it appropriate to do so.

In the week that followed, several resolutions calling for the appointment of a Special Prosecutor were introduced in the Congress. Members of the Senate Judiciary Committee (who were about to consider Richardson's nomination as Attorney General) privately pressed him for an assurance that he would appoint a Special Prosecutor. Some Senators even said publicly that Richardson's confirmation would depend on such an appointment. On May 7, Richardson announced that, if confirmed, he would appoint a Special Prosecutor. The next day Senator Adlai Stevenson, III, introduced a resolution, cosponsored by 23 Democrats, which set forth terms designed to guarantee the independence and authority of a Special Prosecutor.

ESTABLISHING THE JURISDICTION, AUTHORITY AND INDEPENDENCE OF THE SPECIAL PROSECUTOR

Richardson's confirmation hearings, which began on May 9, focused on the terms in the Stevenson resolution he would guarantee and the jurisdiction he would give to the Special Prosecutor. As to jurisdiction, Richardson testified that he would delegate responsibility over the following:

(1) All cases arising out of the 1972 Presidential election campaign including the Watergate break-in case, the Donald Segretti case (Segretti had been charged on May 4 in Florida with fabricating and distributing a letter damaging to three Democratic presidential candidates), and violations of campaign laws;

(2) Cover-up conspiracies and misuse of high Government offices;

(3) The burglary of the office of the psychiatrist of antiwar activist Daniel Ellsberg; and

(4) Procrastination or obfuscation by the Department of Justice, the FBI, or any other agency relating to the cover-up of these cases.

Richardson pointed out that the common denominator of the Special Prosecutor's jurisdiction would be allegations of involvement of White House or CRP officials, or Administration appointees. He said he intended to leave the assignment open in order to delegate matters which at the outset did not seem to be related to Watergate, but which might later prove to be so related. He added that he did not know enough at that time about the milk fund case or the Vesco case to decide whether they should be included, and said that he would deal later with the question of delegating responsibility to investigate various other activities of the White House "Plumbers."

Richardson was equally explicit in his testimony about the authority of the Special Prosecutor. The Special Prosecutor, he stated, would have the necessary financial support to do the job and full authority to select a staff and to exercise the powers normally vested in the Assistant Attorney General in charge of the Criminal Division.[1] In the latter connection, Richardson testified that the Special Prosecutor would be empowered to decide what kind of relationship he would have with various US Attorneys investigating matters under his jurisdiction, including the right to overrule a US Attorney, to intervene at any phase of proceedings being conducted, to dismiss any indictments already brought and to bring more serious charges if he deemed it appropriate.

---

1. Richardson also assured the Committee that he would request the Justice Department and the FBI to detail personnel to the Special Prosecutor's office.

Richardson further stated that he intended to give the Special Prosecutor complete authority to challenge claims of executive privilege (including the right to seek court review)[2] and assertions of the right to withhold information on national security grounds. Richardson also testified that the Special Prosecutor would have the authority to determine if and when to seek a court order granting immunity to a witness.[3]

The question of the Special Prosecutor's "independence" was more difficult. On the one hand, Richardson assured the Committee that the Special Prosecutor would not be removed from office except for malfeasance or gross incompetence. On the other hand, Richardson was faced with the legal obligations which he would assume if confirmed as Attorney General. The Stevenson resolution called for the appointment of a Special Prosecutor with "final" authority. Richardson objected to the use of the word "final"; he felt that statutes giving the responsibility for the administration of the Department of Justice to the Attorney General required that the Attorney General retain ultimate authority. While he said he would delegate "full" authority to the Special Prosecutor, he took the position that he would exercise his ultimate authority only if the Special Prosecutor was "behaving arbitrarily or capriciously." Richardson stressed that he would not interpose his judgment over the Special Prosecutor's in such discretionary

---

2. Since the President's Counsel would represent the White House in such litigation, Richardson said he would not exercise the traditional role of the Attorney General to interpret the applicability of the doctrine of executive privilege.

3. By law (18 USC § 6003), any request by a Federal prosecutor to a court for an immunity order must be approved by the Attorney General, Deputy Attorney General or designated Assistant Attorney General. Richardson said he intended to give approval automatically to any such requests by the Special Prosecutor.

matters as whether to request a grant of immunity, whether to seek an indictment and, if so, on what charges, or whether to take the prosecutorial responsibility out of the hands of a US Attorney. It was Richardson's view that he would be available to consult with the Special Prosecutor, that he would give whatever advice he could and would want to be kept generally informed, but that the Special Prosecutor would not be under any obligation to keep him informed or to seek his approval in advance of a prosecutive decision.

Richardson thought the likelihood of his intervention was so remote as to be practically inconceivable. If it occurred, he said, it would be due to arbitrary action either by the Special Prosecutor or himself; if the latter were true, the Special Prosecutor would have a duty to make the situation known immediately. Richardson further assured the Committee of his support for a full and thorough investigation and suggested that, at some subsequent stage when the Special Prosecutor had substantially completed his job, a panel might be created to review the whole record of the Special Prosecutor's activities.

SELECTION OF ARCHIBALD COX AS SPECIAL PROSECUTOR

On the first day of the hearings Richardson announced that he had consulted 80 to 100 individuals, including the presidents of the American Bar Association and the American College of Trial Lawyers, and had asked them to submit names for the position of Special Prosecutor. He said he would draw up a list, submit it to certain individuals for further comment and then adopt an order in which to approach the persons recommended. He asked the Judiciary Committee to invite the candidates to testify and promised that he would select another if the Committee or the full Senate, by resolution, did not approve his choice.

Richardson was asked and agreed to submit the "final-ists" list to members of the Committee for their comment. He did so after narrowing the list to four persons. On May 15, he announced that the first person on the list was then examining the guidelines drawn up to describe the Special Prosecutor's authority and responsibilities. He told the Committee that he anticipated incorporating suggestions from the candidate and promised to let them know if the top persons turned down the job because they felt there was insufficient flexibility in the guidelines.

Later that day Richardson's first choice, US District Judge Harold Tyler of New York, declined the job. He told the press he thought it would be wrong to resign his judge-ship, particularly in light of the fact that the ground rules were not completely settled. Richardson said he would confer with the remaining candidates before offering the post to anyone. The next day, Warren Christopher, a California attorney and former Deputy Attorney General of the United States, removed himself from consideration after conferring with Richardson. He announced that he had done so because he would not have been granted enough independence.

On May 17, Richardson sent the guidelines for the Special Prosecutor's job to the Judiciary Committee to clarify his position, as refined by the hearings and his inter-views with the candidates for Special Prosecutor. He pledged that he would not countermand or interfere with the Special Prosecutor's decision or actions and would not remove the Special Prosecutor except for extraordinary improprieties. He also announced that he was adding ten names to the list of candidates.

On May 18, Richardson announced that if the Senate approved his own nomination he would appoint Archibald Cox to be the Special Prosecutor. Cox was a professor of constitutional law at Harvard Law School and had served as

Solicitor General of the United States. A final version of Richardson's guidelines—amended to specify that the Special Prosecutor would determine whether and to what extent he would inform or consult with the Attorney General about the conduct of his duties and responsibilities—was presented to the Committee that day. In a separate announcement Cox said he was satisfied that Richardson's guidelines would permit sufficient independence to do the job right. He said that he had studied these guidelines and was satisfied that they gave him all the formal power he needed. As further insurance, Cox agreed to keep a detailed record of his conversations with Richardson and to make a full final report of his work, including factual findings as to high Government officials. Cox said he considered that the "full" authority vested in him was, for all practical purposes, "final," and suggested that the only authority Richardson was retaining was "to give me hell if I do not do the job."

On May 23, the Senate Judiciary Committee voted unanimously to recommend the confirmation of Elliot Richardson. He was confirmed that same day by the full Senate and was sworn in as Attorney General on May 25. Several hours later Cox was sworn in as Special Prosecutor.

ORGANIZATION OF THE WATERGATE SPECIAL PROSECUTION FORCE

On May 31, Richardson issued an order establishing WSPF and setting forth the duties and responsibilities of the Special Prosecutor. He designated Cox as Director of the office and directed all divisions, offices, services and bureaus of the Department of Justice, including the FBI and US Attorneys, to cooperate with the Special Prosecutor on all matters under his jurisdiction.

After Cox had familiarized himself with the factual matters falling within his purview, he met with the Attorney General and Henry Petersen, the Assistant Attorney General for the Criminal Division, to clarify which investigations that the Criminal Division had been handling were encompassed by this mandate. They decided:

- That the Special Prosecutor would be responsible for all cases arising out of the Vesco indictments already returned by the grand jury in the Southern District of New York, but that the Criminal Division, under the supervision of the Special Prosecution Force, would be responsible for the extradition of Vesco;
- That the indictment returned by the Middle District of Florida against Donald Segretti and all cases of campaign violations arising out of the activities of Segretti would be the responsibility of the Special Prosecutor;
- That the Criminal Division would prepare an inventory of all election law cases and investigations then pending with respect to the 1972 Presidential campaign and those Senatorial and Congressional campaigns arguably related to matters within the Special Prosecutor's jurisdiction; the Special Prosecutor would then designate from the inventory those matters over which he would assume total or supervisory responsibility;
- That the Special Prosecutor would be responsible for all matters relating to the burglary of the office of Daniel Ellsberg's psychiatrist;
- That allegations related to the Presidential commutation of Angelo DeCarlo's sentence (DeCarlo had been convicted of extortion) would be investigated by the Special Prosecutor;
- That the Special Prosecutor would be responsible for pursuing any criminal violations in the Department of Justice's settlement of an antitrust case against the

International Telephone and Telegraph Company (ITT); this included possible perjury in testimony before the Senate Judiciary Committee relating to that settlement, and the Securities and Exchange Commission's (SEC) referral to the Justice Department of an allegation that ITT had obstructed an SEC investigation by failing to turn over all relevant documents sought under an SEC subpoena;[4] and

- That the Special Prosecutor would investigate allegations of contributions to the President's campaign by the Lehigh Valley Dairy Association in return for assistance in matters affecting the Association.[5]

---

4. In June 1972 the Senate Judiciary Committee had referred its transcripts of the hearings on the nomination of Richard Kleindienst to be Attorney General—during which much testimony about the ITT antitrust settlement had been given—to the Justice Department for investigation of possible perjury. Shortly thereafter the SEC had referred its subpoena question to Justice. The investigation of these matters had not been completed in June 1973. On June 7, Richardson had asked Cox to take responsibility for the whole matter. Cox had agreed and Richardson had so notified the Chairman of the Senate Judiciary Committee.

5. It was decided that the Criminal Division (1) would handle two investigations already well underway in that Division; (2) would handle the civil cases *Ellsberg* v. *Mitchell* and *Halperin* v. *Kissinger*, charging illegal wiretapping, and would make available to the Special Prosecutor all pleadings before they were filed in the cases; and (3) would answer defense allegations in *US* v. *Briggs* and *US* v. *Ayers* that illegal methods had been used by the White House or the President's campaign committee to obtain evidence against the defendants and would send to the Special Prosecutor copies of all investigative requests to the FBI relating to these allegations and any information thereby developed by the FBI which related to matters within the Special Prosecutor's jurisdiction. In return the Special Prosecutor would send to the Criminal Division any information he developed bearing on these allegations. It was further decided that the Tax Division of the Justice Department would continue to handle potential gift tax violations in connection with political contributions and would advise the Special Prosecutor of violations related to matters within his jurisdiction.

Cox realized that he must organize his office so that it could address new and developing allegations as well as assimilate quickly the vast amount of information which had already been uncovered in matters falling under this jurisdiction. He selected two colleagues from Harvard Law School—Philip Heymann, who had worked for Cox when Cox was Solicitor General, and James Vorenberg, who had served as Executive Director of the President's Commission on Law Enforcement and Administration of Justice[6]—to help him undertake these tasks. In their first days at WSPF, they resolved organizational details with the Attorney General, and established an operating relationship with the Assistant US Attorneys for the District of Columbia who were working on the Watergate investigation, with the Assistant US Attorneys for the Southern District of New York who were handling the Vesco case, and with the FBI. They attempted in the first few days to delay public hearings of the Senate Select Committee on Presidential Campaign Activities and to obtain an inventory, and prevent any possible removal, of documents in the White House files which might be useful to the investigations. During this early period they also recruited staff and supervised the physical establishment of an office.

Cox wanted the WSPF staff to be independent, professional and non-partisan. He felt this was necessary to instill confidence in the public that all allegations would be evaluated and investigated fully and to instill confidence in potential witnesses that their evidence would be weighed seriously and would not be relayed to the Justice Department or to the White House. Although "administratively" his office was part of the Justice Department, he wanted it to function as a separate agency.

6. Stephen Breyer, another Harvard colleague, also joined WSPF for the summer to help organize the ITT task force.

No one from the Justice Department who had had any prior connection with cases within WSPF's jurisdiction or with the White House was hired. Any employee hired from the Department was formally transferred to the staff of the Special Prosecution Force. Cox early decided to establish his own press office rather than to use the Public Information Office of the Department to handle press contacts.

As soon as Cox's appointment was announced, a large number of applications came into his office. By estimate, more than 1,000 applications or expressions of interest came to the new office's attention in the first few weeks. Vorenberg reviewed these and, to fill the senior positions, Cox and he solicited recommendations and evaluations from judges, prosecutors and practicing lawyers. The need to build up a staff quickly required that applicants be available to begin work immediately. A number of those finally selected were known to Cox or Vorenberg through professional or school associations.

From the beginning it seemed clear that the Special Prosecutor's assignments fell into logical divisions and that the office could be organized into "task forces" along those lines. At the same time, because of certain similarities in the areas of investigation, it was recognized that a task force might turn up information of peripheral value which might be significant to another task force's work. Cox anticipated that central coordination and frequent contact among the task forces could minimize the possibility that such information would be neglected. In the first few weeks Vorenberg had principal responsibility for this coordination which was seen as a primary function of the person who would become Deputy Special Prosecutor.

James Neal, a criminal defense lawyer who had served as US Attorney in Tennessee, joined the staff on May 29 to head a task force investigating the Watergate break-in and cover-up. He spent the first few weeks at the District of Columbia US Attorney's office working with the Assistant US Attorneys who had been handling that case. Other early recruits were hired without specific assignments designated for them. Thomas McBride, a former prosecutor and criminal justice administrator, also joined on May 29. He was asked to gather information about several other areas of investigation. He met with the Assistant US Attorney handling the Vesco case and with attorneys from the Criminal Division who were investigating 1972 Presidential campaign contribution reporting violations. He shortly took over responsibility for the campaign contributions task force. Heymann worked with Neal on the Watergate investigation and then shifted to reviewing evidence of illegal activities by the White House Plumbers Unit. James Doyle, a national reporter for the *Washington Star News*, was hired to head the press office.

Thirty days after Cox took office the staff numbered approximately 33 persons, including 21 lawyers. By late June, Cox and Neal became concerned that the lawyers on hand would not be able to assimilate the mass of information being provided daily in testimony before the Senate Select Committee and other Congressional committees. Consequently 10 recent law school graduates were hired and assigned to summarize the Congressional committee transcripts. In addition, Harry Bratt, a career Government administrator with background in computer usage, was hired to study the possibility of computerizing the growing volume of information.

Henry Ruth joined the staff as Deputy Special Prosecutor on July 2. Ruth, a former prosecutor from the Justice Department's Organized Crime Section, had later served as Deputy Director of the Crime Commission, and in 1973 was Director of the New York City Criminal Justice Coordinating Council. As Deputy, Ruth was to supervise the investigations closely and to coordinate the work of the task forces.

Also on July 2, Philip Lacovara, then Deputy Solicitor General of the United States, joined the staff as Counsel to the Special Prosecutor.

By mid-July, William Merrill, a former Assistant US Attorney from Michigan, had been assigned to head the investigation of the "Plumbers" activities; Joseph Connolly, an attorney from Philadelphia, was designated as head of the ITT task force; and Richard David, a prosecutor from the US Attorney's office for the Southern District of New York, was placed in charge of the investigation of Segretti's activities and other campaign "dirty tricks." (Later in the summer Davis took over joint responsibility with Connolly for the ITT task force.) In late July, on Bratt's recommendation, Cox approved the establishment of a computerized Information Section to provide the capability for comparing discrepancies in testimony and for completely cross-referencing subjects and persons mentioned in testimony. The lawyers of the Information Section were assigned to other positions in the office and a paralegal staff was hired and trained for the computer operation.

By the middle of summer 1973, five task forces were in operation. By early September there were 42 lawyers (including four consultants) and 44 other staff members at WSPF. Although there was some staff turnover during the following 18 months and some refinements in the original organizational plan, the office continued with this general structure throughout its tenure, with the abandonment of a task force only upon completion of its work. The office had its highest number of employees in August 1974 when there were 95 staff members.

DISMISSAL OF COX; ABOLITION AND RE-ESTABLISHMENT OF WSPF

The events leading up to the firing of Cox and abolition of WSPF are set out in the principal report. This section describes the period immediately following Cox's firing.

After Acting Attorney General Bork fired Cox, General Haig, of the White House Staff, directed Clarence Kelley, Director of the FBI, to send agents to the WSPF office on the evening of October 20 to prevent removal of any documents. Agents were also dispatched to the Attorney General's and the Deputy Attorney General's offices.

For approximately 16 hours—from 9:05 p.m. on October 20, 1973, to 12:47 p.m. on October 21, 1973— agents of the Federal Bureau of Investigation occupied the offices of WSPF. Although official documents could not be removed, the most important and sensitive documents had been copied earlier in the week after White House counsel Charles Alan Wright hinted in an October 18 letter to Special Prosecutor Cox that if Cox refused to agree to White House compromise proposals on access to Presidential tape recordings, "we will have to follow the course of action that we think in the best interest of the country." Task force leaders and other senior staff members then removed copies of certain items from the office, replacing them when Judge John J. Sirica signed a protective order covering the files on October 26. Copies of documents of a particularly sensitive nature were placed in two safe-deposit boxes in nearby banks.

On the Saturday night of Cox's firing, the Special Prosecutor's staff immediately reported to the office. One of their main concerns was to secure files from anyone who might want to, or be ordered to, read or destroy the files. Since the FBI agent in charge did not have written instructions of his responsibilities and since he said he did not have authority to approve any movement of files within the office, Deputy Special Prosecutor Ruth contacted Henry Petersen, Assistant Attorney General for the Criminal Division of the Justice Department, and received approval to gather the most sensitive papers and place them in front office file safes to which only a few WSPF personnel had the combinations. Ruth also advised Petersen that an important witness was scheduled to testify before the grand jury the following Tuesday and Petersen agreed that that appointment should be kept. Bork gave assurances that the Special Prosecutor's employees were not fired but were to be made employees of the Criminal Division. The staff was advised of these telephone calls and agreed not to take any precipitous action until they had a better understanding of the situation. Around midnight they left the office.

Sometime in the morning hours of October 21, the Justice Department ordered US Marshals to replace the FBI agents occupying the WSPF offices. The marshals arrived at 12:47 p.m. that day.

The next day, a holiday, the staff gathered at the office to assess the situation. Bork announced that Petersen was now in charge of the investigation. That evening Ruth and Lawrence met with Bork and Petersen to discuss the operational relationship between WSPF and the Criminal Division. Ruth agreed to bring each task force to meet with Petersen. Ruth and Lacovara then returned to the office and briefed the staff on the meeting; the staff discussed alternatives and reached no firm conclusions about what it should do.

On Tuesday morning Judge Sirica assured the grand juries that they could rely on the court to safeguard their rights and preserve the integrity of their proceedings. He also scheduled a court hearing on the Presidential tapes at 2 p.m. that day. At the hearing Wright announced that he was not prepared to file a response, but was authorized to say that the President would comply in all respects with the court orders. Shortly, thereafter, Haig announced withdrawal of the offer of summaries of the tapes to the Senate Select Committee.[7]

That same day Bork issued a written order, effective as of October 21, abolishing the Watergate Special Prosecution Force and returning its functions to the Criminal Division. During the next few days Bork and Petersen met several times with Ruth and Lacovara and met once with the full senior staff of the office. Petersen and his assistant John Keeney met with task forces investigating ITT and dairy contributions, and the next week met with the task force investigating the break-in of Daniel Ellsberg's psychiatrist's office.

On October 24, Bork announced that the White House had agreed there should be "regularized procedures" for turning over evidence to the Watergate prosecutors. During that week and the next, draft letters to the White House asking for various records were sent by several task forces to Petersen for his consideration and Petersen and Bork were briefed by Ruth on past difficulties the office had encountered in trying to get documents from the White House.

On October 25, Petersen joined the senior staff in a petition to the District Court for a protective order prohibiting the removal of any grand jury records from the office except by the staff in the course of their work. This request was granted by Judge Sirica the next day; he assigned the General Services Administration the responsibility for ensuring non-removal.

During this week and the next, the normal work of the office, such as interviewing witnesses in the office or in the

---

7. The committee earlier had subpoenaed Presidential tapes for its hearings.

grand jury and requesting the FBI to interview witnesses or obtain documents, was not directly supervised by Petersen, but he was kept informed about major matters. He was briefed on and concurred with the position WSPF was planning to take in further court proceedings over the subpoenaed tapes and Bork approved that the proceedings be handled by WSPF. On October 30 Ruth and Lacovara met with Judge Sirica and White House Counsel Buzhardt to work out the procedures for resolving claims of executive privilege which the President might have with respect to particular passages in the tapes. During the meeting, Buzhardt informed Sirica that two of the subpoenaed conversations had not been recorded. Sirica scheduled a public hearing for the next day to examine the reasons for their non-existence.

On the evening of October 26, President Nixon announced in a press conference that Acting Attorney General Bork would appoint a new Special Prosecutor for the Watergate matter, said that he would not provide any new tapes and documents involving Presidential conversations to the new prosecutor, and indicated that the prosecutor would not be allowed to seek such material through the courts. Softening that position, Haig said on a television program on October 28, that the new Special Prosecutor would not have to pledge not to seek White House tapes and documents.

Over the weekend Bork began calling possible candidates. On October 30, Haig called Leon Jaworski of Houston, Texas, who had served as president of the American Bar Association, and asked him to accept the position; Jaworski agreed to come to Washington the next day to discuss it. Jaworski said he would take the job only if he would be free to bring judicial proceedings if necessary to obtain tapes and other materials he needed. At their meeting Haig left the room and a short time later returned and told Jaworski that the President had agreed that Jaworski would have the right to seek any materials he felt were necessary to carry out his duties and could go to court against the President, if necessary, to obtain such materials. This assurance was then repeated to Bork, White House Counsel Garment and Buzhardt, Petersen, and Senator William Saxbe, whom the President had chosen to be the new Attorney General. Jaworksi accepted the job on the basis of these assurances. No change in the jurisdiction of the Special Prosecutor was discussed.

On November 1, President Nixon announced the nomination of William Saxbe to be Attorney General. Bork then announced the appointment of Jaworski. He said that Jaworski would have the same charter as Cox had had and said that the President had given his personal assurance that he would not exercise his right to fire the Special Prosecutor without first obtaining the consensus of the majority and minority leaders of the House and Senate and the chairmen and ranking members of the House and Senate Judiciary Committees. An order in accordance with this assurance was issued by Bork the next day.

Jaworski was sworn in as Special Prosecutor on November 5. That afternoon he addressed the entire staff of WSPF, then met with the senior staff, and then with Cox, Ruth and Lacovara. He began his duties promptly by meeting the next day with each of the task forces to review their investigations.

REACTION TO COX'S FIRING AND LEGISLATIVE PROPOSALS TO ESTABLISH A SPECIAL PROSECUTOR

Cox's press conference on October 20 had been televised nationally. Following it, and greatly increasing after the resignation of Richardson and the firing of Cox and Ruckelshaus were announced, the public overwhelmingly expressed support for Cox and dismay at President Nixon's actions.[8] Many insisted that the President comply with the court orders, resign or be impeached. On October 22, NBC News reported that a scientific sampling poll conducted since the night of October 20, showed 44 percent of Americans favored impeaching Nixon, 75 percent opposed the dismissal of Cox, 48 percent thought Nixon should resign, and 54 percent thought Watergate should not be "put behind us."

Labor leaders, lawyers, newspapers, and others called for the President's resignation or impeachment. Ralph Nader announced that he would file a lawsuit challenging the firing of Cox. The president of the American Bar Association, Chesterfield Smith, called on the courts and the Congress to take appropriate action, including but not limited to creation of a new Special Prosecutor independent of the executive branch. Various protest marches and rallies were held.

Hearing of the resignation and firings, the Senators who had been drawn into the tapes issue also were dismayed. Senator Baker said he was shocked and had not known in advance that President Nixon was planning to forbid Cox to pursue his court quest. Senator Ervin said he did not see where his and Baker's tentative agreement with the President to accept verified transcripts of taped conversations would have any relation whatever to Cox or his work.

---

8. The public reaction was reflected in telephone calls, telegrams, and letters to the White House, the Congress, and other Government agencies. On October 23, Western Union announced that its Washington office had been inundated and that three high-speed teleprinters had been installed in Virginia to handle the backlog. Over 160,000 telegrams had been received. By October 29, over 350,000 telegrams had been sent to Washington on this issue in the preceding nine days.

Senator Stennis, the proposed verifier, said that he had not been told that Cox had rejected the President's proposal.

On October 22, the Associated Press polled 75 House members and found 44 for impeachment and 17 undecided. The few House Democratic leaders who were in Washington over the holiday weekend met and tentatively agreed that the House Judiciary Committee should make a preliminary investigation to determine whether there were grounds to impeach President Nixon. They also discussed whether Congress could, constitutionally, create a Special Prosecutor post in the executive branch completely independent of presidential control. They scheduled a meeting with the full leadership for the next day to discuss these issues further. The Senate Judiciary Committee scheduled a meeting for October 24, to decide whether to conduct a hearing on the resignation and firings.

On the morning of October 23, House Republican leaders met with Presidential Adviser Bryce Harlow and told him that they would not try to block impeachment proceedings unless the President made the Watergate tapes available to the District Court. They also urged appointment of a new Special Prosecutor. When the House convened at noon that day, Gerald Ford announced, on behalf of the Republican leaders, that they had no objection to the Democratic plan to refer impeachment resolutions to the House Judiciary Committee. Already that morning seven such resolutions had been so referred.

That same morning Elliot Richardson held a nationally televised press conference at the Department of Justice. While refusing to charge President Nixon with failure to respect the claims of the investigative process, Richardson declared that in going to the Department of Justice his single most important commitment to helping restore the integrity of the governmental processes was his pledge to the independence of the Special Prosecutor and that he could not be faithful to that commitment and also acquiesce in the curtailment of the Special Prosecutor's authority. He said that in Cox's shoes he would have done what Cox had done, and he said he thought a new Special Prosecutor should be appointed.

After the 2 p.m. announcement that the President would turn the subpoenaed tapes over to Judge Sirica, Haig and Wright held a press conference at the White House to explain the reversal. Haig gave the President's reasons for having sought the compromise: polarization within the body politic, with the threat of impeachment and the possibility that the President might be removed with no Vice President in office; the intensification and prolongation of debate if the President appealed the case to the Supreme Court; and suspicion of disunity by any foreign leader calculating the unity, permanence, strength, and resilience of this Government. Calling the President's proposal that Stennis listen to and report on the tapes "a herculean effort to resolve the constitutional crisis" and "a fundamental concession in the national interest," Haig said that when Cox defied the President by challenging the proposal the President had no alternative but to dismiss him.

Denying that President Nixon had decided before the previous week to dismiss Cox because his office was making its investigations broader than the President considered proper, Haig said that "many of us" were concerned about the political alignment of Cox's staff, that it was roaming outside its charter, and there had been occasions, before the dispute of the previous week, when the President was not pleased with Cox's conduct.[9] Haig indicated that the

9. In his October 20, 1973, press conference, in referring to his telephone call from Wright on the evening of October 18, Cox said: "It was my impression that I was being confronted with things which were drawn in such a way that I could not accept them."

President would adhere to his plan to put the Watergate case within the institutional framework of the Department of Justice.

This plan was strongly opposed by many members of Congress. On October 23, establishment of an independent Special Prosecutor was proposed in two House bills, one calling for appointment of the prosecutor by majority vote of the House and Senate, the other calling for appointment by the Chief Judge of the Court of Appeals. In the Senate two bills for appointment of a Special Prosecutor by the Chief Judge of the District Court were introduced and referred to the Judiciary Committee.

Throughout the week House Republican leaders met with Bryce Harlow and White House lawyers to implore them to persuade President Nixon to name a new Special Prosecutor in order to forestall the legislation. Senate Republican leaders urged the same and agreed that if President Nixon declined they would support (or would not oppose) legislation under which the District Court would do so.

The President's announcement on October 26, that he would have Bork appoint a new Special Prosecutor did not relieve Congressional pressure for a statutorily created prosecutor. Both the House and the Senate Judiciary Committees began consideration of such legislation the following week. Cox appeared before the Senate Committee on October 29, 30 and 31 to describe his former staff, his jurisdiction, his progress, and his unsuccessful efforts to obtain documents from the White House. He urged legislation to create an Office of Special Prosecutor with District Court appointment of the prosecutor, jurisdiction at least as broad as he had had, and specified standing to invoke judicial process to obtain evidence. The House Judiciary's Subcommittee on Criminal Justice began its hearings on October 31 and heard legislators, lawyers, and law professors support various legislative proposals.

Notwithstanding the announcement on November 1, of Jaworski's appointment, both the Senate Judiciary Committee and the House Judiciary Subcommittee on Criminal Justice continued their hearings on the Special Prosecutor legislation.

Bork testified before the House Subcommittee on November 5, that any such legislation could be unconstitutional and indicated that he might advise the President to veto it. He pointed out that defendants could go free if the legislation were found unconstitutional and that witnesses and evidence could be lost in the delays for testing the law's constitutionality. He emphasized the Special Prosecutor's independence as assured by Haig and by the Congressional "consensus" clause in the new Special Prosecutor charter. Bork was followed by Cox who told the Subcommittee that he felt the overriding concern was continuing the Watergate investigations. Thus, prompt action on either a statute for District Court appointment of a new Special Prosecutor or one for Presidential appointment with approval of the Senate was more important than which of the two methods was chosen.

Richardson testified before the Senate Judiciary Committee on November 6 and 8. He reiterated the practical reasons he had given in his nomination testimony for establishment of a Special Prosecutor only within the executive branch and suggested appointment of a new prosecutor by President Nixon with confirmation by the Senate. He also called for a commitment by the President to waive executive privilege with respect to any Presidential materials the Special Prosecutor needed and suggested that the Senate might hold up their confirmation of Saxbe as Attorney General until the President made such a commitment.

On November 8, Jaworski testified before the House Subcommittee that passage and legal testing of a statute providing for appointment of a Special Prosecutor outside the executive branch would delay the effective work of his office for an extended period of time and that he had what he considerred all of the independence that could be expected by a Special Prosecutor. He stressed the unqualified assurances he had received from Haig, after Haig had consulted with the President, that there would be absolutely no constraints on his freedom to seek any and all evidence and to invoke judicial process should he consider it necessary.

The Subcommittee then drafted, and on November 12, referred to the full Judiciary Committee, a bill under which a Special Prosecutor would be appointed by a panel of three judges of the District Court, and removed only by that panel and only for gross dereliction of duty, gross impropriety, or physical or mental inability to discharge his powers and duties. The Special Prosecutor would have all of the jurisdictional and functional authority that the previous Special Prosecutors had had, would report annually to the panel, the Attorney General, and the Congress, and would serve for a term of three years.

On November 14, Bork testified before the Senate Judiciary Committee, reiterating the practical problems and constitutional questions that he had voiced before the House Subcommittee as to the Special Prosecutor legislation. He emphasized the important safeguard that the Congressional consensus clause added to the Special Prosecutor's independence and explained that, although he had not spoken to the President personally about it, he considered the President's knowledge that he was going to include the clause to be the President's personal assurance and a moral commitment by the President to the Congress and the American people. Bork explained that, in addition to dismissal, the consensus requirement related to any attempt to limit the Special Prosecutor's power.[10]

The final witness before the Senate Judiciary Committee was Jaworski, who testified on November 20. He emphasized the strength of the assurances he had received from Haig and from the charter re-establishing the Prosecution Force. Jaworski explained that he thought his charter included all of the matters he thought he should have under his jurisdiction and that if he came upon some matter which he thought he should investigate which was not included he would ask the Attorney General for its inclusion. He pointed out that Bork had told him he was completely independent from any obligation to report to or to seek the advice or counsel of the Attorney General.

The House Judiciary Committee reported its Subcommittee's Special Prosecutor bill to the full House on November 26, with an additional provision that the Special Prosecutor report at least monthly, to the chairman and ranking minority of the Committee, any information pertinent to whether impeachable offenses had been committed by Richard Nixon. The Senate Judiciary Committee, divided equally, reported two bills to the full Senate on December 3, one similar to the House bill and the other providing for appointment of a Special Prosecutor by the Attorney General after consultation with Senate leaders and prohibiting removal of the prosecutor without the consensus of certain congressional leaders. None of the bills was enacted into law.

A further opportunity for the Senate to consider the independence and authority granted to the Special

---

10. This aspect was not clear in the charter. On November 19, Bork issued an amendment specifying that the jurisdiction of the Special Prosecutor would not be limited without the consensus of the designated members of Congress.

Prosecutor under the charter prepared by Bork was afforded to the Senate Judiciary Committee in the November 1973 hearings on the nomination of Saxbe to be Attorney General. Saxbe pledged that Jaworski would operate completely freely and Saxbe would see him only at Jaworski's request, that he would give Jaworski any reasonable assistance he could furnish from the Justice Department, and that he would inform the Committee of any White House attempt to limit the jurisdiction or to tamper with the charter of the Special Prosecutor. Jaworski promised to bring any impasse to the attention of the Congressional "Committee of Eight" designated in his charter and the Judiciary Committees of the House and Senate.

CIVIL SUIT AGAINST COX'S DISMISSAL

On October 23 Ralph Nader and other co-plaintiffs filed a civil suit against the firing of Archibald Cox with Acting Attorney General Bork named as defendant. On October 29, Nader filed a motion to have Cox reinstated as the Special Prosecutor and to have the Watergate investigations halted until Cox reassumed control. On November 9, Judge Gesell dismissed Nader as a plaintiff, stating that Nader clearly lacked the legal standing to bring such a suit, declined to order Cox reinstated, noting that Cox had not entered the case or otherwise sought reinstatement, and declined to halt the investigations, noting that a new Special Prosecutor had been sworn in and that the public interest would not be served by placing restrictions on his investigations.

On November 14, Gesell found that the firing of Cox, in the absence of a finding of extraordinary impropriety as specified in the regulations establishing the Office of Watergate Special Prosecutor, was illegal, that that regulation barred the total abolition of the Special Prosecutor's office without the Special Prosecutor's consent, and that even if the regulation did not bar total abolition without that consent, its revocation under the circumstances presented in this case was arbitrary and unreasonable and was, therefore, illegal. Gesell called the abolition and reinstatement of the office under a virtually identical regulation "simply a ruse to permit the discharge of Mr Cox without otherwise affecting the office of the Special Prosecutor." As to the legality of Leon Jaworski's service, Gesell held that Bork's actions in appointing a new Special Prosecutor were not themselves illegal since Cox's decision not to seek reinstatement necessitated the prompt appointment of a successor to carry on the important work in which Cox had been engaged.

New titles in this series

The War Facsimiles

The War Facsimiles are exact reproductions of illustrated books that were published during the war years. They were produced by the British government to inform people about the progress of the war and the home-defence operations.

The Battle of Britain, August–October 1940

On 8 August 1940, the Germans launched the first of a series of mass air attacks on Britain in broad daylight. For almost three months, British and German aircraft were locked in fierce and prolonged combat in what has become known as the Battle of Britain. In 1941 the government published *The Battle of Britain* to explain the strategy and tactics behind the fighting that had taken place high in the sky over London and south-east England. Such was the public interest in this document, with its graphic maps and photographs, that sales had reached two million by the end of the war.

ISBN 0 11 702536 4   Price £4.99 US $8.95

The Battle of Egypt, 1942

Often referred to as the Battle of El Alamein, this battle was one of the major turning points for the Allies in World War II. The British, commanded by General Montgomery, were defending Egypt while the Germans under Rommel were attacking. This was a campaign the British could not afford to lose, because not only would it leave Egypt wide open for invasion, but it would also mean the loss of the Suez Canal and the oil fields. First published in 1943, *The Battle of Egypt* is an astonishing contemporary report of one of the most famous military victories in British history.

ISBN 0 11 702542 9   Price £5.99 US $10.95

Bomber Command: the Air Ministry account of Bomber Command's offensive against the Axis, September 1939–July 1941

Churchill declared on 22 June 1941: "We shall bomb Germany by day as well as by night in ever-increasing measure." Bomber Command of the RAF was to translate those words into action, beginning its attacks on Germany in May 1940, and steadily increasing its efforts as the war progressed. Published in 1941 at the height of World War II, *Bomber Command* tells the story of this fighting force during those early years.

ISBN 0 11 702540 2   Price £5.99 US $11.95

East of Malta, West of Suez: the Admiralty account of the naval war in the eastern Mediterranean, September 1939 to March 1941

This is the story of the British Navy in action in the eastern Mediterranean from September 1939 to March 1941 and their bid to seize control. During this time British supremacy was vigorously asserted at Taranto and Matapan. This facsimile edition contains contemporary maps, air reconnaissance photographs of the fleets and photographs of them in action.

ISBN 0 11 702538 0   Price £4.99 US $8.95

Fleet Air Arm: the Admiralty account of naval air operations, 1943

The Fleet Air Arm was established in 1939 as the Royal Navy's own flying branch. With its vast aircraft carriers bearing squadrons of fighter pilots, its main role was to protect a fleet or convoy from attack, or to escort an air striking force into battle. In *Fleet Air Arm*, published in 1943, the public could read for the first time of the expeditions of these great ships as they pursued and sank enemy warships such as the *Bismarck*.

ISBN 0 11 702539 9   Price £5.99 US $11.95

Land at War: the official story of British farming
1939–1944

Land at War was published by the Ministry of Information in 1945 as a tribute to those who had contributed to the war effort at home. It explains how 300,000 farms, pinpointed by an extensive farm survey, had been expected to increase their production dramatically, putting an extra 6.5 million acres of grassland under the plough. This is a book not just about rural life, but of the determination of a people to survive the rigours of war.

ISBN 0 11 702537 2   Price £5.99 US $11.95

Ocean Front: the story of the war in the Pacific,
1941–44

Ocean Front tells the story of the Allies' war against Japan in the central and western Pacific. Starting with Pearl Harbor in December 1941, this fascinating book recounts the Allies' counter-offensive, from the battles of the Coral Sea and Midway, to the recapture of the Aleutian Islands and the final invasion of the Philippines. Illustrated throughout with amazing photographs of land and sea warfare, *Ocean Front* provides a unique record of the American, Australian and New Zealand fighting forces in action.

ISBN 0 11 702543 7   Price £5.99 US $11.95

Roof over Britain: the official story of Britain's
anti-aircraft defences, 1939–1942

Largely untold, *Roof over Britain* is the story of Britain's ground defences against the attacks of the German air force during the Battle of Britain in the autumn of 1940. First published in 1943, it describes how the static defences – the AA guns, searchlights and balloons -- were organised, manned and supplied in order to support the work of the RAF.

ISBN 0 11 702541 0   Price £5.99 US $11.95

Uncovered editions: how to order

FOR CUSTOMERS IN THE UK
Ordering is easy. Simply follow one of these five ways:

Online
Visit www.clicktso.com

By telephone
Please call 0870 600 5522, with book details to hand.

By fax
Fax details of the books you wish to order (title, ISBN, quantity and price) to: 0870 600 5533.
Please include details of your credit/debit card plus expiry date, your name and address and telephone number, and expect a handling charge of £3.00.

By post
Post the details listed above (under 'By fax') to:
The Stationery Office
PO Box 29
Norwich NR3 1GN
You can send a cheque if you prefer by this method (made payable to The Stationery Office). Please include a handling charge of £3 on the final amount.

TSO bookshops
Visit your local TSO bookshop (or any good bookshop).

FOR CUSTOMERS IN THE UNITED STATES
Uncovered editions are available through all major wholesalers and bookstores, and are distributed to the trade by Midpoint Trade Books.
Phone 913 831 2233 for single copy prepaid orders which can be fulfilled on the spot, or simply for more information.
Fax 913 362 7401